GOLD, DOLLAR, AND EMPIRE

Francisco Soberón Valdés

Spanish edition first published in 2010, *Oro, dólar e imperio*

ISBN-13: 978-1519489814

Library of Congress Control Number: 2015920013

First English Edition

Copyright © 2016 by Francisco Soberón Valdés

ISBN: 1519489811

ABOUT THE AUTHOR

Francisco Soberón worked in shipping between 1961 and 1978. During that period he represented Cuban shipping companies in Canada, Holland, and the United Kingdom and served on the board of directors of the Caribbean Multinational Shipping Company, which had headquarters in San José, Costa Rica.

From 1978 to 1995, he headed shipping, insurance, and financial companies in London, Cuba, and the Netherlands Antilles and served as a member of the Baltic Exchange, London, and of the Latin American Committee of Lloyds Register of Shipping.

From 1995 to 2009 he was governor of the Central Bank of Cuba, and he intervened in several international events, including summit of ECOSOC, IMF, and World Bank, United Nations, 1999; Annual Meeting of the Bank for International Settlements, Basel, Switzerland, 1996, 1998, and 2001; Conference on International Finance and Development, Monterrey, Mexico, 2002; Seminar on Latin-American Integration, Caracas, 2006; General Assembly of the Latin-American Association of Financial Institutions, Havana, 2006; and Meetings of the Unitary System of Regional Payments, Caracas, 2009.

He has traveled to more than fifty countries, including trips as an adviser on shipping and financial subjects to Angola, Nicaragua, Vietnam, Venezuela, and São Tomé and Principe.

He has written several essays and articles for newspapers and ten books in the Spanish language: *Fletamento de buques* (1984); *Fomento de la flota mercante propia* (1987); *Financiación y compra de buques*

(1989); *Finanzas, banca y dirección* (2000); *Martí: el poder de servir* (2009); *Finanzas internacionales y crisis global* (2009); *Oro, dólar e imperio (Gold, Dollar, and Empire) (2010); El laberinto monetario global* (2012); *El euro: unión monetaria y crisis* (2014); and *Diccionario de términos e instituciones del Sistema Financiero Internacional* (2015).

FOREWORD

Toine Knipping, CEO of Amicorp; author of *Mind Your Business: Thoughts for Entrepreneurs*

G old, Dollar, and Empire presents a treasure trove of empirical data on the relationship between a nation's wealth and its power. In a matter-of-fact tone, Francisco Soberón uses the history of gold and the gold standard to illustrate in an unambiguous manner how over the course of history countries have amassed gold and financial reserves and used them to further their economic and geo-political goals. The golden rule in the reality of our humanity usually turns out be "who has the gold gets to make the rules'.

The principle that power corrupts and absolute power corrupts absolutely is presented for the financial theatre in a masterful way. Cruel leaders and regimes over the ages are replaced only to see new leaders and regimes also turn cruel. Economic policy is a power struggle with money as one if its main weapons.

Mr. Soberón is a humble man. For fifteen years he was the Governor of the Central Bank of Cuba, and in that during the 'Special Period' after the disappearance of the Soviet Union in the 1990's was instrumental in keeping the Cuban economy afloat against great odds.

Mr. Soberón has significant firsthand experience of how economic and monetary power is used in the ongoing power struggles between nations. Cuba, being a small and economically weak power has often been on the losing end of such struggles. Nevertheless, he never turned cynical or defeatist. As Gold, Dollar, and Empire also illustrates, there comes an end to every economic hegemony over time. The empires of Alexander the Great, The Spanish, Dutch and British Empires all came to their end when they consistently started spending significantly more than they were producing.

It makes one wonder about the next chapter in history. There is a clear and present worldwide shift taking place in economic power and wealth. From the First World War until the Vietnam War the USA seemed to be destined to be the world's dominant economic power forever. A few years ago we were all led to believe that the BRIC's would be the great new economic powers. Now China has become the largest economy in the world and the country with the largest financial reserves.

And of the other BRICs, only India is showing great economic progress. Countries with high savings rates, who prioritize investments in infrastructure and production capacity over greater individual spending power, are destined to take over from countries with greater consumption for personal purposes or military adventures. The new-found economic strength of China, India and other Asian powers has not yet been reflected in similar political and military clout, but it is obvious that eventually greater economic power will be followed by increasing political might and a shift in the balance of power towards Asia.

PREFACE

The present text is a condensed version of my book *Oro, dólar e imperio* (in the Spanish language), published in 2010.

Its main objective is to provide data and assessment about the background of the events that led the world to the present monetary system, through reviewing the historical process during which the dollar gradually took the place of gold as the center of the global monetary system.

As the global crisis that started in 2007 has demonstrated, the present monetary system is inherently weak. It does not contribute to the normal functioning of international economic relations, and if no action is taken, it is likely to cause new episodes of turbulence that could lead to new severe and profound crises.

Considering the importance of this subject and its impact on the internal economies of most countries of the world, it is very important to constantly provide new sources of information and analysis about it so that as many people as possible become aware of the roots of the present international monetary system and its potential risks. This book modestly aims to be part of that effort.

CONTENTS

CHAPTER 1

Conquering Gold

Historians relate that when Alexander the Great conquered Susa in 331 BCE he brought in more than three hundred tons of gold from the royal treasury there, and he added more at other points along his route in Persia; he used this gold mainly to mint coins.[1]

He also arranged for the existing coins to be melted back into his own money in the coin workshops of the conquered regions. Consequently, his coins circulated in a much larger area than any other currency ever before. These circumstances contributed to the economic expansion in the Eastern Mediterranean region during what is known as the Hellenistic Period 323 BCE–31 BCE).

After Alexander's empire disintegrated, the structure of the coinage in the Hellenic realms remained fairly uniform. More than one hundred years after his death in 323 BCE, these coins were still circulating. The last coins bearing Alexander's name were minted around 65 BCE.[2]

In 202 BCE, during the second Punic War, the Romans won access to the gold-mining region of Spain, which provided them with an important source of this precious metal. As a result of a victory in the Gallic Wars (58 to 51 BCE), Julius Caesar brought back enough gold to give a substantial number of coins to his soldiers and pay Rome's debts.[3]

15

Francisco Soberón

Around 794–796, Charlemagne defeated the Avars and penetrated their inner fortress, called the Ring, where they had accumulated vast quantities of gold during centuries of conquests and plunder. As a result of this victory, he seized substantial quantities of gold, which he distributed among the clergy, nobles, soldiers, and his kingdom in general, all of which helped him to consolidate his power.

During his fourth voyage to America, Christopher Columbus wrote a letter to the Spanish king and queen that left no doubt regarding the enthusiasm that gold provoked in him. He said, "Gold is most excellent. Gold constitutes treasure, and he who possesses it may do what he will in the world, and may so attain as to bring souls to Paradise."[4]

The Spanish conquerors melted and cast into coins many gold objects that were priceless treasures of the New World's culture. Historians differ about the exact quantity of gold that Spain received from its colonies in America during the sixteenth century, but they believe it to be approximately between 150 and 300 metric tons. After a hazardous voyage through the Atlantic Ocean—during which the fleet had to face not only the elements but also the dangerous actions of pirates and corsairs—this gold was minted and used to cover the imports and other expenses of the Spanish crown. About 70 percent of these expenses were linked to Spain's frequent wars.[5] A great quantity of the imports came from Great Britain, which for many years served as the main producer of manufactured goods to the rest of the world.

Something similar happened in relation to the gold that came in to Portugal from Brazil. An important part of it was sent to Great Britain, to pay for British products and for those of other European nations that received their payments through Britain.[6]

So a substantial part of the gold Spain and Portugal obtained from their colonies in the New World found its way to British banks. There it became part of the support for the eventual establishment of the gold standard in that nation.

In the first half of the nineteenth century, there was a great demand

16

in Great Britain for Chinese goods such as tea, silk, and porcelain. China did not experience a similar demand for British goods, so British merchants had to pay with silver. To obtain that silver, Britain would have had to affect its gold reserves. In order to save its gold, Britain instead decided to pay with government-produced opium from India, a British colony at that time. When the Chinese emperor prohibited the import of opium because of the very negative costs of opium addiction to the Chinese society, the British Crown decided to resort to its powerful navy to force the Chinese emperor to accept the import of opium. According to a prestigious British historian, the Chinese Emperor "was about to feel the full force of history's most successful narco-state: the British Empire."[7] As a result of the so called "Opium Wars" that followed, China was forced to accept the import of opium through five of its main ports, to deliver Hong Kong to Britain, and to pay very high cash indemnities in silver. In very short words, the British Empire, to preserve its gold reserves, resorted to war in order to legalize drug trafficking and use drugs to pay for its imports from China.

It is estimated that South Africa has been the source of about 34 percent of the gold produced in the world, and it possesses a great part of the world's reserves of this precious metal. Great Britain not only supplied most of the funds needed to develop gold mining in South Africa, but it also kept a great part of the gold that was refined in London and sold it to the Bank of England and to other London financial agents.[8]

It is then not surprising that Great Britain retained control over South Africa for such a long time. At the moment of the cruelest repression of the Apartheid regime, when hundreds of students were killed in Soweto during 1976 and 1977, the IMF—with the support of the United States, the United Kingdom, Germany, and Italy—provided more credits to South Africa than to the rest of the African countries combined.[9]

The above are only a few cases that show how gold, due to its very special properties and in particular to its monetary use, has been present since ancient times in the history of the greatest empires and the wars they fought. Early peoples always highly appreciated gold because of its scarcity, durability, and enticing appearance. The Egyptians considered it to be a divine and indestructible metal associated with the brilliance of the sun. They even believed that their gods had golden skin. "Dr. Freud relates that there are peculiar reasons deep in our sub consciousness why gold in particular should satisfy strong instincts and serve as a symbol. The magical properties, with which Egyptian priestcraft anciently imbued the yellow metal, it has never altogether lost."[10] From the beginning of civilization, gold was an attractive metal that was monopolized by the upper classes and heavily concentrated in palaces and temples of the ancient world. Gold is the most malleable and ductile of all known metals. By the early seventeenth century, a troy ounce of gold could be beaten to nearly fourteen square meters, and at present this can be done to eighteen square meters and even more.[11]

Gold Monetary Qualities

As regards the question of why gold and silver, and no other commodities, were used since remote times as the monetary material it is difficult to find a better explanation than the one given by Karl Marx in the middle of the nineteenth century. He pointed out that in order to function as a measure of value, a commodity first has to express purely quantitative differences, thus presupposing identical, homogeneous quality. He summarized this condition as follows:

If, for instance, one evaluates all commodities in terms of oxen, hides, corn, etc., one has in fact to measure them in ideal average oxen, average hides, etc., since there are qualitative differences between one ox and another, one lot of corn and another, one hide and another.

Gold and silver, on the other hand, as simple substances are always uniform and consequently equal quantities of them have equal values. Another condition that has to be fulfilled by the commodity which is to serve as universal equivalent and that follows directly from its function of representing purely quantitative differences, is its divisibility into any desired number of parts and the possibility of combining these again, so that money of account can be represented in palpable form too. Gold and silver possess these qualities to an exceptional degree.

As means of circulation gold and silver have an advantage over other commodities in that their high specific gravity—representing considerable weight in a relatively small space—is matched by their economic specific gravity, in containing much labour-time, i.e., considerable exchange-value, in a relatively small volume. This facilitates transport, transfer from one hand to another, from one country to another, enabling gold and silver suddenly to appear and just as suddenly to disappear—in short these qualities impart physical mobility, the sine qua non of the commodity that is to serve as the perpetuum mobile of the process of circulation.

The high specific value of precious metals, their durability, relative indestructibility, the fact that they do not oxidise when exposed to the air and that gold in particular is insoluble in acids other than aqua regia—all these physical properties make precious metals the natural material for hoarding...

Metals in general owe their great importance in the direct process of production to their use as instruments of production. Gold and silver, quite apart from their scarcity, cannot be utilized in this way because, compared with iron and even with copper (in the hardened state in which the ancients used it), they are very soft and, therefore, to a large extent lack the quality on which the use value of metals in general depends. Just as the precious metals are useless in the direct process of production, so they appear to be unnecessary as means of subsistence, i.e., as articles of consumption. Any quantity of them can thus be placed at will within the social process of circulation without impairing production and consumption as such. Their individual use-

value does not conflict with their economic function. Gold and silver, on the other hand, are not only negatively superfluous, i.e., dispensable objects, but their aesthetic qualities make them the natural material for pomp, ornament, glamour, the requirements of festive occasions, in short, the positive expression of supra abundance and wealth. They appear, so to speak, as solidified light raised from a subterranean world, since all the rays of light in their original composition are reflected by silver, while red alone, the colour of the highest potency, is reflected by gold. Sense of colour, moreover, is the most popular form of aesthetic perception in general. The etymological connection between the names of precious metals and references to colour in various Indo-European languages has been demonstrated by Jakob Grimm (see his History of the German Language*).*

Finally the fact that it is possible to transform gold and silver from coin into bullion, from bullion into articles of luxury and vice versa, the advantage they have over other commodities of not being confined to the particular useful form they have once been given makes them the natural material for money, which must constantly change from one form into another...

Gold and silver are not by nature money, but money consists by its nature of gold and silver.[12]

Summarizing, gold has the required properties to fulfill the functions of money. Its stock is limited, at least in the short run, because of its scarcity and high cost of production. It is durable, easily recognizable, storable, portable, divisible, and standardizable. As regards gold's remarkable properties, some further interesting observations can be made.

As Marx explained, gold represents a considerable weight in a relatively small cubic size. Half a ton of gold measures only one cubic foot. Therefore, at the prices prevailing at the beginning of 2016 (about 1,100 dollars per troy ounce), one cubic foot of gold has a value of around 17.5 million dollars. (One metric ton equals 32,150.7 troy ounces.)

Gold has always been a very scarce metal. According to several reliable sources, the total quantity of gold mined during the whole history of humanity is about 170,000 metric tons, which a big modern bulk carrier could transport in a single voyage, using only part of its capacity. About two-thirds of this amount has been mined in the last sixty-five years. It is estimated that about 15 percent of that gold has been lost, whereas the remaining 85 percent still exists in some form. It is estimated that there are reserves of about fifty-five thousand metric tons of minable gold still in the ground.[13]

Regarding gold's durability, there is a very interesting recent example. Since 2007, there has been a legal dispute between a US treasure-hunting company and the Spanish government about the ownership of 594,000 gold and silver coins worth around five hundred million dollars, belonging to the Spanish frigate *Nuestra Señora de las Mercedes*, a Spanish vessel sunk by a British squadron off Cape St. Mary, Portugal, in October 1804. Probably all metal objects of that ship had been totally destroyed after lying at the bottom of the ocean for two centuries, whereas the gold coins were recovered and have kept all their qualities, despite being exposed to such an aggressive environment for all that time.[14]

In addition to its monetary functions, gold has many industrial uses, of which the most significant quantitatively is in electronics circuitry. A report of the U.S. Department of Interior and the U.S. Geological Survey, indicates that modern solid-state electronic devices use very low voltages and currents and that in such low-energy electronic circuitry, electrical continuity is easily interrupted by the development of oxide films or other tarnishing films on critical circuit components. They conclude that gold properties make it invaluable in these circuits because they help in retaining a low, constant contact resistance during long periods of time in hostile environments. Gold also has other very important industrial uses and "plays a prominent role in space exploration. The electronics of the space vehicles, obviously the kinds of devices that must be absolutely dependable, incorporate gold in crucial circuitry, and since mechanical parts also must function dependably they too require the unique properties of gold. For example, conventional organic lubricants are not suitable for the lubrication of moving parts in space because they are too volatile in the near-vacuum and are degraded by the intense radiation encountered... In these situations, gold, which has a very low shear strength, has been used as a solid film lubricant for moving parts in space vehicles."[15] Gold is also used in other important functions related to space-exploration programs.[16]

Origin of the Monetary Use of Gold

According to reliable historians, gold bars were already used as a medium of exchange in the fourth millennium BCE. By 1500 BCE, the gold-rich regions of Nubia had made Egypt a wealthy nation, and gold became the recognized standard medium of exchange for international trade. As a matter of fact, the use of bars for common transactions has many inconveniences, including the need to weigh the gold to assess its exact value, since a very small difference in volume could mean a significant amount in terms of its value. On the other hand, the bar could also be adulterated with less valuable metals.

The first coins of silver and gold were minted in Lydia (east of Turkey) in the seventh century BCE. Coins had the advantage of being easier to handle, to keep, to carry, and to use in daily transactions than the bigger, heavier, and less handy bars. These first Lydian coins were made of electrum (gold-silver alloy); they were irregular in size and shape but were minted according to a strict weight standard. Electrum coinage soon spread to the Greek cities of coastal Asia Minor and then to the Greeks of the islands and the mainland.[17]

After the appearance of these first coins, the concept of coinage spread to other places in Europe, and silver was the metal most used for European coinage. In the second and first centuries BCE, the Roman senate granted Roman generals the right to strike coins from captured silver and gold so they could pay their soldiers. A Roman general in

Asia Minor, L. Cornelius Sull, struck a gold "aureus" to commemorate a victory—the first Roman gold coin struck in quantity. Julius Caesar continued his military right to strike coins after becoming dictator of the empire in the late first century BCE. His aureus was the first Roman gold coin not struck out of necessity, and it made circulating gold coinage more common. In the first century CE, Emperor Nero further expanded gold coinage by continuing to strike an aureus and adding a gold quinarius, which had half the value of an aureus. Both coins used almost pure gold and were issued in large quantities. During the Middle Ages in Western Europe, gold coins were an important part of the continent's development. In the 1200s, Venice and Florence in Italy were principal cities for world trade. Venice issued a gold *ducat* coin, and Florence issued a gold *florin* coin. Both coins were widely accepted in international trade. The *ducat* became the standard European currency for about five centuries.[18] The history of humanity shows us that for many centuries there have been continual changes in the decisions as to which precious metal should predominate in the monetary system.

"For hundreds, even thousands, of years the choice of mankind has wavered undecided between gold and silver. The chief cause of this remarkable phenomenon is to be found in the natural qualities of the two metals. Being physically and chemically very similar, they are almost equally serviceable for the satisfaction of human wants. For the manufacture of ornaments and jewellery of all kinds the one has proved as good as the other."[19] To summarize this very ancient "dispute," the fact is that silver alone, or together with gold as part of bimetallism, prevailed until the second half of the nineteenth century, when gold finally won this centuries-long battle for monetary supremacy.

According to the writings of John Maynard Keynes, *"Some four or five thousand years ago the civilized world settled down to the use of gold, silver, and copper for pounds, shillings, and pence, but with silver in the first place of importance and copper in the second. The Mycenaeans put gold in the first place. Next, under Celtic or Dorian influences, came a brief invasion of iron in place of copper*

23

over Europe and the northern shores of the Mediterranean. With the Achaemenid Persian Empire, which maintained a bimetallic standard of gold and silver at a fixed ratio (until Alexander overturned them), the world settled down again to gold, silver, and copper, with silver once more of predominant importance; and there followed silver's long hegemony (except for a certain revival of the influence of gold in Roman Constantinople), chequered by imperfectly successful attempts at gold-and-silver bimetallism, especially in the eighteenth century and the first half of the nineteenth, and only concluded by the final victory of gold during the fifty years before the war."[20]

As far as the relationship between the values of silver and gold is concerned, the latter has always been a much more valuable metal than silver. This relationship has varied from about six to one in ancient Asia, fifteen or sixteen to one during the Roman Empire, and around fifteen to one in the eighteenth century and the first half of the nineteenth century. Afterward, this relationship has kept moving in favor of gold, and at present it is around seventy-five to one.

Because of the characteristics and attractions of gold and its monetary use, since ancient times monarchs have been in control of the mines where it was produced. Criminals and slaves were doing the hard, physical work of mining the metal. When monarchs started to mint their own money, they soon realized that they could obtain additional profits by reducing its weight or debasing it, altering its gold or silver content. In connection with this idea, Adam Smith said the following:

By means of such expedients the coin of, I believe, all nations has been gradually reduced more and more below its original value, and the same nominal sum has been gradually brought to contain a smaller and a smaller quantity of silver. Nations have sometimes, for the same purpose, adulterated the standard of their coin; that is, have mixed a greater quantity of alloy in it...The adulteration of the standard has exactly the same effect with what the French call an augmentation, or a direct rising of the denomination of the coin. An augmentation, or a direct rising of the coin, always is, and from its nature must be, an open and avowed operation. By means of it pieces of a smaller weight and bulk are called by the same name which had before been given to pieces of a greater weight and bulk. The adulteration of the standard, on the contrary, has generally been a concealed operation. By means of it pieces were issued from the mint of the same denominations and, as nearly as could be contrived, of the same weight, bulk, and appearance with pieces which had been current before of much greater value. When King John of France, in order to pay his debts, adulterated his coin, all the officers of his mint were sworn to secrecy. Both operations are unjust. But a simple augmentation is an injustice of open violence, whereas the adulteration is an injustice of treacherous fraud...

In the end of the reign of Henry VIII and in the beginning of that of Edward VI the English coin was not only raised in its denomination, but adulterated in its standard. The like frauds were practiced in Scotland during the minority of James VI. They have occasionally been practiced in most other countries.[21]

It is easy to understand that such adulteration in the metal contained within gold and silver coins helped monarchs and feudal lords in Europe to finance their frequent and costly wars, for which they incurred very high expenses, but which produced future income only if victory could be obtained, an outcome that was always uncertain. This adulteration is one of the reasons a discrepancy arises between the current monetary names based on various weights of precious metals and the actual weights that those names originally represented. Other reasons included the import of foreign money into an imperfectly developed community, as in Rome in its early days, where gold and silver coins circulated first as foreign commodities. The names of these foreign coins never coincide with those of the indigenous weights. They also included the change from less-precious metal to the more precious, as a measure of value; for instance, silver replaced copper, and gold replaced silver. The word *pound*, for example, was the monetary name given to an actual pound (in terms of weight) of silver. When gold replaced silver as a measure of value, the same name was applied according to the ratio between the values of silver and gold, to perhaps one-fifteenth of a pound of gold. The word *pound*, as a monetary name, thus becomes differentiated from the same word as a weight-name. The fact that the currency of coins itself effects a separation between materials' nominal and real weight creates the basis for the possibility of replacing metal coins with simple symbols—like paper money, which could perform the same functions.[22]

Paper Money and Fiat Money

Paper was first produced in China. Thus, it is not surprising that paper money first appeared in China in the ninth century. Its appearance was associated with the growing need for metallic currency, the lack of enough coins to match this growth in demand and the inconvenience of carrying very large quantities of metal coins over very long distances.

It is said that at the end of the Tang period, traders deposited their valuables with their corporations and received bearer notes. The authorities exploited this idea and invited merchants to deposit their metallic money in the government Treasury. In exchange, the authorities offered official "compensation notes," called *Fey-thsian*, or *flying money*.

Marco Polo was amused at the thought that, whereas the alchemists had tried to turn base metals into gold, the Chinese emperors had very simply turned paper into money. However, when he informed people about this on his return home, they were very skeptical about this experience.[23]

In Western Europe paper money appeared during the Middle Ages, and there it was also related to the difficulties in using metal coins for trade and the activities of the first European bankers. Later on, monarchs decided on a convenient system that allowed them to keep the precious metals in their treasuries and use paper to perform the regular functions of money. Nevertheless, paper money represented a fixed amount of gold or silver and could be exchanged at any time for such amount.

For a very long time, commercial banks issued paper money. England, which was the most advanced capitalist country, entrusted the authority to issue paper money for England and Wales only to the Bank of England in 1844, although Scottish banks kept their prerogative to issue their own bills. In other countries the centralization of money issuing happened many years later. At the time of the foundation of the German central bank in 1875, thirty-one *notenbank* in Germany issued their own money. In Japan the Central Bank was established in 1871, and it obtained the right to be to sole issuing bank of the country only in 1882. In the United States by the time of the Civil War, an estimated 7,000 different bank notes were circulating, the issue of some 1,600 different state banks.[24]

With the development of monetary systems, what prevails at present is the fiat money, which has no intrinsic value and cannot be converted into any precious metal but is legal tender, by order of the national governments. Analyzing the difference between gold coins and paper money, Karl Marx pointed out that in the circulation of tokens of value, all the laws governing the circulation of real money seem to be reversed and turned upside down, since gold circulates because it has value, whereas paper money has a value because it circulates.

Summarizing, in an historical context, we first had money that was in itself a valuable object, such as precious metal. Afterward, paper money was backed by holdings of gold or silver and could be converted into it at a fixed price at any time. Finally, we developed paper money not backed by anything other than the government's decision to make it legal tender. This last concept prevails in our times, especially since the collapse of the Bretton Woods agreements in 1971.[25]

Francisco Soberón

Notes and Bibliography

(1)   This amount seems a little exaggerated, since the total gold mined by humanity till 1850 added up to only about ten thousand metric tons. (Timothy Green, *El nuevo mundo del oro* [Barcelona: Editorial Planeta S. A., 1983], 19.) However, there is no doubt that the quantity of gold that Alexander the Great obtained from his campaigns in Persia was substantial and of great significance to his kingdom.

See W. C. Butterman and Earle B. Amey III, *Mineral Commodity Profiles-Gold* (Reston, VA: US Department of the Interior, US Geological Survey, 2005), 4.

(2)   See Nina Van Meerbeeck, *Alexander the Great: Between god and man* (National Bank of Belgium Museum); see also Kenneth Matziorinis, A Brief History of the International Monetary System (Montreal: McGill University, 2006), 6.

An essay of the World Gold Council states, *"Gold was just as central to ancient Greece as ancient Egypt, but in a way that seems more familiar to us today—as a primary financial commodity. By 550 BC, the Greeks had started mining for gold throughout the Mediterranean and Middle East regions... According to Greek mythology, Agamemnon was king of Mycenae and the leader of the Greek expedition to Troy. He is believed to have lived around 1550 BC. A gold funerary mask excavated at Mycenae by the German archaeologist Herinch Schliemann in 1876, is reputed to be his... By 325 BC the Greeks had mined in areas from Gibraltar to Asia Minor and Egypt and would soon begin to practice alchemy— the quest to turn base metals into gold. Considering that gold is an element, the alchemists were of course never successful, but their efforts are clear evidence of gold's ongoing mystique and desirability."* (World Gold Council, The Ancient World (pre 400 AD), page 2.)

(3)   See World Gold Council, *The Ancient World (pre 400 AD)*.

(4)   "Christopher Columbus, Letter from the Fourth Voyage," https://earlyamericas.wordpress.com/.../columbus-letter-from-the-fourth-voyage/

(5)   See Harold Kirkemo et al., Gold (Denver: US Geological Survey), 7; see also John Kenneth Galbraith, *Historia de la Economía* (Barcelona: Editorial Ariel S.A., 1991), 46. In Civilization, Niall Ferguson mentions that in Peru the Spanish conquerors obtained 13,420 pounds of 22-karat gold at a stroke when Atahualpa delivered it to them in a vain attempt to obtain his liberty. Niall Ferguson, *Civilization* (New York: The Penguin Press, 2011). 101.

(6)   See Adam Smith, *An Inquiry into the Nature and Causes of the Wealth of Nations*, http://www.feedbooks.com,70.

(7)   Niall Ferguson, *The Ascent of Money* (New York: The Penguin Press, 2008), 289–291.

(8)   See Timothy Green, *El Nuevo mundo del oro* (Barcelona: Editorial Planeta, S.A., 1983), 48.

(9)   See Anthony Sampson, *Los Bancos y la Crisis Mundial* (Barcelona: Economía y Empresa, Grijalbo, 1984), 221–222.

(10)   John Maynard Keynes, *Essays in Persuasion* (New York: Harcourt, Brace, and Company, 1932), 182.

(11)   See W. C. Butterman and Earle B. Amey III, *Mineral Commodity Profiles-Gold* (Reston, VA: US Department of the Interior, US Geological Survey, 2005), 3; see also Robert A. Mundell, *The International Monetary System in the 21st Century: Could Gold Make a Comeback?* (Columbia University).

(12)   Karl Marx, A *Contribution to the Critique of Political Economy*, (Moscow: Progress Publishers, Online Version: Marx.org, 1993, Marxists.org, 1999); see also Michael David Bordo, *The Classical Gold Standard: Some Lessons for Today* (St. Louis: Federal Reserve Bank, 1981), 1.

(13)   See John M. Lucas, *Gold, Mineral Year Book* (Washington: US Bureau of Mines, 1993), 399; see also Ed Prior, *How much gold is there in the world?* (BBC News, April 1, 2013); see also Mineral *Commodity Summaries* (US Geological Survey, January 2015).

(14)   See Giles Tremlett, "Treasure from sunken galleon must be returned to Spain, judge says," *The Guardian*, February 1, 2012.

(15)   Butterman and Amey, *Mineral Commodity Profiles*, 33–37.

(16)   A seldom-mentioned aspect of gold production is its negative impact on the environment. For an ore grade (i.e. metal content) of 3.5 grams per metric ton of ore, it is estimated that production of one metric ton of gold from nonrefractory ore uses approximately 200,000 gigajoules (GJ) of energy and 260,000 metric tons of water. It produces 18,000 metric tons of GHGs (CO_2 equivalent) and 1,270,000 metric tons of waste solids. For refractory ores, the GHG emissions and energy use are about 50 percent higher, owing to the additional processing steps required. See European Commission DG Environment News Alert Service, *Science for Environment Policy*, edited by SCU (Bristol: The University of the West of England).

Francisco Soberón

(17)   See The British Museum, *Explore/Money.* See also Edwin Walter Kemmerer, *Oro y Patrón Oro* (Buenos Aires: Editorial Sudamericana, 1947).

(18)   See *The history of gold coins,* http://www.numismaster.com/ta/inside_numis.jsp see also Kenneth Matziorinis, *A brief History of the International Monetary System* (Montreal: McGill University, 2006), 8.

(19)   Ludwig von Mises, *The Theory of Money and Credit* (Library of Economics and Liberty), 1.1.12.

(20)   Keynes, *Essays in Persuasion,* 181–182.

(21)   Adam Smith, *An Inquiry into the Nature and Causes of the Wealth of Nations,* 825–826.

(22)   See Karl Marx, *Capital,* Volume I, 68 and 82.

(23)   See Coralie Boeykens, *Paper money, a Chinese invention?* (National Bank of Belgium).

(24)   See John Kenneth Galbraith, *Money: Whence it came, where it went* (London: Penguin Books, 1989), 98.

(25)   See Karl Marx, *A Contribution to the Critique of Political Economy* (Moscow: Progress Publishers, Online Version: Marx.org, 1993, Marxists.org, 1999). See also http://lexicom.ft.com.

CHAPTER 2

Characteristics and Rules of the Gold Standard

A lthough it is common to talk about the gold standard as a single system, in fact we could clearly identify at least four different kinds of gold standards.[1]

Pure Gold Standard, in which an authority buys and sells gold in unlimited quantities at legally fixed prices. This means that anyone can go to that central authority (central bank, government mint, etc.) with coins and acquire gold bars or vice versa. As a matter of fact, the authority must keep reserves of gold large enough to fulfill this obligation. Gold coins circulate in unlimited quantities, and there are no restrictions in holding gold, selling and buying it internally, or importing or exporting it.

Classical Gold Standard, which functions on the same basis as the pure gold standard, except that bank notes that represent a legally established fixed quantity of gold also circulate (together with gold coins). These bank notes are redeemable in gold according to their face value as fixed by the law. This system prevailed at the international scale from the 870s until 1914. During this period of time, paper money gradually replaced gold coins. It is estimated that gold coins declined from about 20 percent of the world's money supply in 1800 to 10 percent in 1913 and to almost zero in 1928. It should be clarified that the zero figure does not mean that gold coins did not exist at that time but that they were mainly used as reserves for treasuries, central banks, and—to a lesser extent—for commercial banks.

Gold *Bullion Standard*, which was proposed by David Ricardo in 1816 and adopted in Great Britain after more than one century, between 1925 and 1931. The rules are the same as those of the classical gold standard, but gold coins do not circulate, and paper money is not redeemable in gold coins. However, the central bank or similar authority has an obligation to buy and sell gold bars without restriction at a price fixed by law. This alternative substantially reduces the selling of gold by these authorities, considering the high value of a gold bar. For example, in the above-mentioned period (1925-1931) in Great Britain the standard weight of a gold bar was 400 ounces, with a price of about 1,700 pounds sterling or 8,300 dollars[2] (this amount of dollars in 1930 had the same buying power as 118,000 dollars in 2015 according to the inflation calculations of the United States Department of Labor). Therefore, only people or institutions that could afford this amount of cash could buy gold bars, which definitely reduced the demand for this precious metal. Normally only banks or important commercial and financial companies required gold on such a scale.

Gold Exchange Standard, in which the national paper money replaces all the monetary functions of gold, and the central bank or similar monetary authority has no obligation to sell gold in exchange for the national paper money in circulation. Instead, they sell – at a fix rate of exchange - foreign currency of a country which is obliged to convert it into gold at a fixed price. This alternative enables a nation to keep its currency at parity with gold without having to keep large reserves of this metal. This is a very convenient system for countries—such as Great Britain or the United States—which issue the most important convertible currencies, since other countries accumulate large amounts of foreign-exchange reserves in sterling and dollars. This amounts to a very cheap source of financing for these two countries, since those reserves are usually deposited in their banks or invested in their public debt, generally at very low interest rates.

Under the gold standard, money supply depends on gold reserves.[3]

When a country has a persistent deficit in its balance of payments, gold will flow out. *(In very simple terms, the balance of payment is a summary of the transactions of a country with the rest of the world for a certain period of time).* If gold outflows exceed gold inflows, the money supply will diminish, and this will cause a downward pressure on prices, which in turn will result in domestic goods becoming cheaper than imported goods. In such circumstances, falling internal prices will lower the prices of domestic goods in foreign countries, increasing exports. All this will contribute to eliminate the deficit in the balance of payments.

On the contrary, when a country has a surplus in the balance of payments, gold inflows will exceed gold outflows, the money supply will increase, prices will go up, domestic goods will be less competitive in export markets, and the higher prices will make domestic goods less competitive in relation to imported goods. Then imports will increase, exports will decrease, and the surplus in the balance of payments will disappear.

According to the rules of the game, central banks have to facilitate international-payments adjustment, either by reinforcing the effects of payment imbalances on the domestic economy so as to speed up the adjustment process, or at least by not hindering those effects. When there is a balance-of-payment deficit, centrals banks have to use discount rates and other monetary tools to deflate the economy until the equilibrium is restored, and if there is a surplus, they have to be willing to inflate prices.[4]

Evidence indicates that historically many central banks did not follow these "rules of the game," considering the disruptions they could mean for the immediate functioning of the national economy. Nevertheless, from 1870 until 1914, the system of fixed exchange rates was maintained, with its positive effect of stability on international trade and finance. As a general rule, countries agreed to the principle of giving priority to the convertibility of the currency as opposed to any internal macroeconomic target. The gold standard had extended at the world level, and there was what some authors call an ideology and practice of orthodox metalism. Furthermore, the system was firmly backed by Great Britain, which was by that time the center of the commercial and financial world.

Evolution of the Gold Standard till World War II

The specific types of gold standard that prevailed in different time periods and places are difficult to establish, although we do know dates that signal important events like its collapse in 1914 and its restoration during the thirties.

According to Keynes,

Whilst gold as a store of value has always had devoted patrons, it is, as the sole standard of purchasing power, almost a parvenu. In 1914 gold had held this position in Great Britain de jure over less than a hundred years (though de facto for more than two hundred), and in most other countries over less than sixty.[5]

In any case, by the eighteenth century the gold standard was already established in practical terms in Great Britain, and in 1816 it was legally established in that country. During the 1870s it was adopted by the most important countries, such as France, Belgium, Switzerland, Germany, and the Scandinavian countries. Russia also joined this group in 1898.

Great Britain helped influence the continuous growth in the group of countries that adopted the gold standard. By that time, this nation —which was considered the center of that system—was, by far, also the center of the commercial and financial activity of the world. It was producing more than 30 percent of global GDP; its energy consumption was five times that of the United States and Prussia and 155 times that of Russia. It accounted for one-fifth of the world trade, and all this with about two percent of the world's population.[6] Furthermore, in 1893 British capital invested abroad made up about 15 percent of all British wealth.

In 1914, fifty-nine countries had implemented the gold standard: a great number of European countries, Canada, the United States, many South American countries, and most Asian nations, with the important exception of China, which stuck to the silver standard till 1935.

It should be noted that among the principal countries in the second half of the nineteenth century, only the United States produced gold and silver, which supplied a source of wealth to support its economic development. Western European countries received almost all their gold and the major part of their silver from Australia, Mexico, Russia, and South America.

The stability that prevailed in the international monetary system till 1914 ended because of the political crisis that finally caused World War I. In September of that year, Great Britain abandoned the gold standard.

That was an unavoidable decision, since at the end of 1913 almost half of the world's foreign-exchange reserves were in pounds sterling, but the Bank of England had only 3 percent of the world's gold reserves.[7]

An interesting piece of information highlights the critical point British finances reached at that time: the economic adviser Sir George Paish wrote a letter to the Chancellor of the Exchequer explaining that the Bank of England could count on a total of around fifty-five million pounds sterling of gold, whereas deposits in the banking system exceeded 1.15 billion pounds. So if only around 5 percent of deposit holders wanted to convert their money to gold, the whole of the gold reserves of the Bank of England would disappear. Sir George warned that if the confidence was not maintained, a large part of the gold in the Bank of England would probably disappear in a few days, and specie payments would have to be suspended.[8]

The information about the size of the deposits and the small amount of reserves backing them clearly shows the benefit that accrued to Great Britain's position as center of the financial world at that time. The system allowed the country to obtain a very cheap source of financing, by taking foreign deposits that were not backed by its metallic reserves.

Once Britain dropped the gold standard, other countries followed, and with the start of World War I, the gold standard collapsed on an international scale. In 1917, the United States prohibited exports of gold and went off the gold standard as far as international transactions were concerned.[9]

During World War I, the political and military situation in Europe helped to increase the flow of gold to the United States, which in 1913 had already accumulated 27 percent of the world's reserves of gold.

Gold Standard between the Two World Wars

At the end of World War I, the world economy had substantially changed. Before 1914 the United States had been considered as a rapidly growing young economy with large deficits in its current account. A small part of that deficit was usually covered by gold exports and the greatest part by an inflow of foreign capital.

As a result of World War I, the evolution of the United States from a capital import economy to an exporter of capital accelerated and experienced a great leap forward. It began to emerge as the world's strongest country. Its exports grew three fold, and its income due to the export of services—mainly maritime transport—doubled.

In belligerent nations, governments largely replaced individuals as the major traders on international markets. These nations exercised a great demand for American goods and created an excess of exports from the United States. This excess was paid first by gold and afterward by credits that the United States extended to its European allies. Those capital movements transformed the international investment position of the United States from a net debt of 3.7 billion dollars in 1914 to a net credit of the same amount by the end of 1919.

As soon as hostilities ceased, the effort to organize a new international monetary system began. The prevailing idea was to return to the times of stability associated with the gold standard, during which prices did not experience substantial changes. There were cyclical variations, and during wars prices experienced disruptions, but currency was backed by gold or silver, and over the long term prices went up and down mainly as a result of changes in the supply of these two metals. The long-term rate of inflation—as we know it in present times—was basically zero.[10]

In order to find ways to confront the state of distress of the European economy after the war, and to return to the stability of prices and rates of exchange of the prewar times, an International Financial Conference was held in Brussels in 1920, attended by thirty-nine countries. This conference considered a viable gold standard as an ideal scenario but pointed out that countries should not attempt to achieve it before reaching internal financial stability and becoming ready to do so.

Two years later, an Economic and Financial Conference was held in Genoa. Efforts to coordinate policies ended in failure, but countries adopted a recommendation that would have far-reaching consequences for the international monetary system. The conference called to economize on the use of gold by maintaining reserves in the form of foreign balances. Central banks were urged to desist from the competitive struggle for gold and maintain their main reserves in the convertible currency of the stronger countries—at that time Great Britain and the United States—whereas these two countries should maintain their reserves mainly in gold.

This recommendation, implemented under the auspices of the League of Nations, was instrumental in the establishment of the gold exchange standard in many countries that returned to the convertibility of their currencies. As a result, the United States and Great Britain obtained the great privilege of concentrating most of the gold reserves and obtaining cheap credit in terms of the deposits of dollars and sterling that other countries kept as part of their international reserves.

As a clear consequence of this recommendation, international reserves, which in 1913 had amounted to 4.5 billion dollars, 4,000 in gold (89 percent), and 500 million in foreign currency (11 percent) had substantially changed in quantity and composition by 1928. At that time they amounted to 9.25 billion dollars, 6 billion in gold (65 percent), and 3.25 billion (35 percent) in foreign currency. In other words, the participation of foreign exchange in the composition of total international reserves increased by 24 percentage points, and gold decreased in the same proportion. Furthermore, the currencies of the two above-mentioned nations formed 98 percent of the foreign exchange, 77 percent in sterling and 21 percent in dollars.[11]

Although the pound kept a predominant role, its replacement by the US dollar was only a matter of time. The United States continuously increased its gold reserves as compared to a Great Britain, whose influence in the international economy was already decaying. As a clear example, by 1928 the United States was already holding about 37 percent of the world's gold reserves, whereas Great Britain held only 7 percent.

In 1924, Germany returned to the gold standard as part of its stabilization plan to stop the hyperinflation that was sinking the country into political and economic chaos.

In 1925, Britain also came back to the gold standard, fixing the rate of exchange to the US dollar through the respective dollar content of these two currencies at 4.86 dollar-pound, similar to the rate in place before World War I. This decision was strongly criticized because of its adverse effects on economic growth and employment, in so far as it overvalued the pound by around 10 percent and made British exports less competitive, with consequent negative results for the balance of payments.

The most prominent British economist at that time, John Maynard Keynes, strongly rejected this alternative. He called the gold standard a *barbarous relic*, explaining that when stability of the internal price level and stability of the external exchanges were incompatible, the former was generally preferable. He pointed out that the restoration of the gold standard (whether at the prewar parity or at some other rate) would not give Great Britain complete stability of internal prices and could only give it complete stability of the external exchanges if all other countries also restored the gold standard. He also pointed out that under the circumstances prevailing after World War I, gold had become a *managed* currency, the future course of which almost entirely depended on the policy of the Federal Reserve of the United States. He finally concluded, "Since I regard the stability of prices, credit, and employment as of paramount importance, and since I feel no confidence that an old-fashioned gold standard will even give us the modicum of stability that it used to give, I reject the policy of restoring the gold standard on prewar lines. At the same time, I doubt the wisdom of attempting a 'managed' gold standard jointly with the United States...because it retains too many of the disadvantages of the old system without its advantages, and because it would make us too dependent on the policy and on the wishes of the Federal Reserve Board."[12]

France and Belgium restored the gold standard in 1926, and Italy did so one year later. In general, in the twenties the countries of greatest economic importance in the international economy also followed that route. In some cases they opted for the gold bullion standard and in others for the gold exchange standard.

Countries largely returned to the gold standard with the idea that this was the best action to achieve price stability, increase international trade, win the confidence of the investors, and stimulate economic growth. However, the *kingdom of gold* in this case did not last very long.

At the beginning of the thirties, Great Britain, which was still an important country as far as international trade and finance were concerned, was again facing a very difficult situation. It suffered all the consequences of the depression that had started at the end of the twenties with its devastating effects in the financial markets and the real economy. Most European debtors lacked the necessary resources to reimburse their debts to Great Britain, in such a way that the financial flows to that nation diminished at a moment when they were badly needed, as deposits and other sterling liabilities reached very high levels.

On the other hand, the already mentioned overvaluation of the sterling pound was having a very negative effect in British exports, contributing to the increase of unemployment that came as a consequence of the Great Depression. Unemployment reached a peak of 21 percent of the total labor force.

These were well-known facts to sterling holders, who were afraid that British authorities could not keep backing their obligations in gold. Therefore, sterling holders exchanged their pound assets for gold, creating an unbearable liquidity situation. As a result of those fears, in the course of a few weeks the Bank of England paid out two hundred million pounds sterling in gold or its equivalent, which was about half the total claims of foreigners on London. It did this at a time when the sums that London had re-lent abroad were largely frozen.[13]

Finally, in September 1931, the Bank of England had to suspend the convertibility of sterling into gold, at a time when only 130 million pounds sterling in gold remained in the bank vaults. By all measures that amount was insufficient to meet the liabilities that were being realized. Sterling depreciated against gold about 48 percent over the next two months.[14]

The Situation in the United States: The Decisions of President Roosevelt

In the United States, as the economic crisis was worsening, President Roosevelt decided to tighten his control on gold. For that purpose, on April 5, 1933, he issued Executive Order 6102, requiring gold coin, gold bullion, and gold certificates to be delivered to the government.

This executive order prohibited the hoarding of gold coin, gold bullion, and gold certificates within the continental United States by individuals, partnerships, associations, and corporations.

It required all people and entities to deliver on or before May 1, 1933, to a Federal Reserve Bank or a branch or agency thereof, all gold coin, gold bullion, and gold certificates then owned by them or coming into their ownership on or before April 28, 1933, except for such amount of gold as could be reasonably required for legitimate and customary use in industry, profession, or art; gold coin and gold certificates in an amount not exceeding in the aggregate one hundred dollars belonging to any one person; gold coins having a recognized special value to collectors of rare and unusual coins; and gold coin and bullion earmarked or held in trust for a recognized foreign government, foreign central bank, or the Bank for International Settlements. The gold bullion delivered to the Federal Reserve was paid at the official price of 20.67 dollars per troy ounce. This executive order further stated that whoever willfully violated any of its provisions might be fined not more than ten thousand dollars, or, if a natural person, might be imprisoned for not more than ten years, or both; and any officer, director, or agent of any corporation who knowingly participated in any such violation could be punished by a like fine, imprisonment, or both.

Meanwhile, the economic international scenario was deteriorating because of the world depression. Former president of the United States Hebert Hoover had promoted an international conference to try to find solutions to the economic problems and to reach some agreement to stabilize foreign-exchange arrangements. The World Monetary and Economic Conference finally convened in London in June 1933, but by that time President Roosevelt had already decided to proceed according to the national interests of the United States, without too much coordination with other countries. He sent a message to the conference dissociating the United States from any attempt to achieve any temporary and probably artificial stability in foreign exchange on the part of a few large countries. The Conference was a total failure.[15]

It was evident that the United States was trying to keep all alternatives open so they could take whatever action they deemed appropriate to achieve their specific goals, without taking into consideration other countries' views.

On October 22, 1933, in his regular radio program, President Roosevelt made some other important announcements regarding his gold policy. He explained that because of events in other parts of the world and internal conditions, the United States needed to control the gold value of the dollar.

He pointed out that the dollar was too greatly influenced by the accidents of international trade, by the internal policies of other nations, and by political disturbances in other continents. He concluded that the United States should take in its hands the control of the gold value of the dollar, to prevent dollar disturbances from hampering the recovery of commodity prices.

He then made the following statement: "I am going to establish a Government market for gold in the United States. Therefore, under the clearly defined authority of existing law, I am authorizing the Reconstruction Finance Corporation to buy gold newly mined in the United States at prices to be determined from time to time after consultation with the Secretary of the Treasury and the President. Whenever necessary to the end in view, we shall also buy or sell gold in the world market. My aim in taking this step is to establish and maintain continuous control." He explained that this step was not simply intended to offset a temporary fall in prices and emphasized that the United States was moving toward a managed currency.[16] Following this decision, the dollar prices kept fluctuating till January 1934, when the Gold Reserve Act was passed.

This act confirmed the prohibition on holding gold, established by the Executive Order of April 5, 1933. Under its terms, ownership of all monetary gold held by individuals and institutions, including the Federal Reserve, was transferred to the Treasury Department. The act prohibited the Treasury and financial institutions from redeeming dollars for gold, contrary to the system that had prevailed since the nineteenth century. Under that system, the government converted paper currency to gold coins whenever citizens desired to do so. After this act, the government converted gold into dollars, regardless of whether citizens wanted to engage in the exchange.

The act also regulated the use of gold. For example, monetary gold had to be held as bars. Coins were forbidden. Bars could be obtained for certain industrial uses, whereas gold items could be bought and sold if they weighed less than fifteen ounces, but transactions for heavier items required licenses.

The act authorized the president to fix the weight of the gold dollar at any level between 50 and 60 percent of the prior legal weight. Under this authority, the president fixed the buying and selling price of gold at thirty-five dollars per troy ounce, thereby devaluing the gold dollar to 59.06 percent of the value set by the Gold Act of 1900, which equaled $20.67 per ounce. That rate had prevailed until the spring of 1933, when the Roosevelt administration began its campaign to devalue the dollar, as has already been indicated.

By valuing its own gold holdings at $20.67 per troy ounce and paying that price for the gold it acquired from private individuals and entities, the Treasury realized a profit of a nominal value of about three billion dollars. It used part of this profit to establish a stabilization fund of two billion dollars that could be used to buy or sell gold, foreign currencies, financial securities, and other financial instruments in order to control the dollar's value.

As a matter of fact, all individuals and entities that had been obliged to sell their gold to the Treasury at $20.67 per ounce saw the gold value of the dollars they received reduced to 59 percent of their previous value. The same happened to those who maintained deposits or held cash in dollars.

After February 1, 1934, the official price of gold remained fixed at thirty-five dollars per troy ounce in such a way that it marked the date of the return of the United States to the gold standard. However, this gold standard was different from the one it had left less than a year earlier, as the mint bought all gold offered at the price of thirty-five dollars per troy ounce but sold only for the purpose of foreign payments. As already pointed out, the holding of gold and bullion was forbidden to private individuals except for use in industry and art, and numismatic holdings and gold no longer circulated domestically.[17]

The price fixed for gold initially overvalued the product and stimulated a rapid increase in the production and accumulation of gold in the United States. Gold production in this country rose from less than 2.6 million ounces in 1933 to 6 million in 1940. Furthermore, the gold policy of President Roosevelt coincided with an important increase of capital flows from Europe to the United States, since Hitler came to power in January 1933 and the fear of war was growing. Under these circumstances, gold holders considered the United States to be a safe place to keep their wealth. For these reasons, the US share of the world's stock of gold rose from 38 percent in 1929 to 71 percent in 1939.[18]

The US ban on citizen gold ownership was in force for forty-two years. It ended in January 1975, when the government lifted this restriction and gold could again be freely held in the United States without any licensing or restrictions of any kind. Citizens of this country were again free to hold gold in any form and amount they could afford. Notwithstanding this prohibition, it is estimated that at the time this ban was raised, wealthy American citizens were holding about 4,000 to 4,500 metric tons of gold abroad, particularly in Switzerland.[19]

As a result of the world depression and the abandonment of the gold standard by Great Britain and other countries, many currencies were continuously devalued, in order to make national products more competitive and to increase exports. These competitive devaluations created a very unstable situation, which was extremely negative for the normal development of international trade and the economy in general. In this scenario, the three most important countries in world trade and finance at that time, France, Great Britain, and the United States, met in 1936 to try to stabilize their currencies.

As a result of this meeting, these three countries signed a Tripartite Agreement, pledging to refrain from competitive devaluation and to maintain currencies at existing levels as long as that attempt would not interfere seriously with internal prosperity. This accord contributed to reduce the fluctuation of these currencies during the next three years.[20]

The political tensions arising before World War II made the economic situation increasingly unstable and made it impossible to achieve any serious coordination to find real solutions to the severe crisis that the world was experiencing at that time. Finally, World War II started, and many countries established official fixed exchange rates for their respective currencies. At this stage the rates were based in strict exchange-control arrangements that limited free transactions in foreign exchange and gold.[21]

Francisco Soberón

Notes and Bibliography

1)   Actually, I have found that experts on this subject refer to gold standards in the following nine manners: managed, pure coin, mixed, orthodox, classic, bullion, exchange, specie, and unrestricted. See among others Michael David Bordo, *The Classical Gold Standard: Some Lessons for Today* (St. Louis: Federal Reserve Bank, 1981), 1; Lawrence H. Officer, "Gold Standard," in *EH.Net Encyclopaedia*, ed. Robert Whaples (Chicago: University of Illinois, 2008), 8; Edwin Walter Kemmerer, Oro y Patrón Oro (Buenos Aires: Editorial Sudamericana, 1947), 19; Ian Shannon, *International Liquidity* (Melbourne: F. W. Cheshire Pty Ltd, 1964), 4; *The Key to the Gold Vault* (New York: Federal Reserve of New York, 2008), 5.

2)   See Lawrence H. Officer, "Gold Standard," in *EH.Net Encyclopaedia*, ed. Robert Whaples (Chicago: University of Illinois, 2008), 9-10.

3)   Referring to the limits that the metallic backing of currency imposes on the normal functioning of the capitalist system, Karl Marx pointed out, "With the development of the credit system, capitalist production continually strives to overcome the metal barrier, which is simultaneously a material and imaginative barrier of wealth and its movement, but again and again it breaks its back on this barrier." Karl Marx: *Capital*, Volume III, 407.

4)   See John Dutton, *The Bank of England and the Rules of the Game under the International Gold Standard: New Evidence*, 174, http://www.ber.org. chapters/ c11128. See also Ian Shannon, *International Liquidity*, Melbourne: F. W. Cheshire Pty Ltd, 1964), 6.

5)   John Maynard Keynes, *Essays in Persuasion* (New York: Harcourt, Brace, and Company, 1932), 181–182.

6)   See Fareed Zacaria, *The Post-American World* (New York: W. W. Norton and Company, 2008), 174.

7)   "An official run on sterling could easily force Britain off the gold standard. Because sterling was an international currency, private foreigners also held considerable liquid assets in London, and could themselves initiate a run on sterling." Lawrence H. Officer, "Gold Standard," in *EH.Net Encyclopaedia*, ed. Robert Whaples (Chicago: University of Illinois, 2008), 17.

8)   See Marcello de Cecco, *The International Gold Standard* (London: Frances Pinter, 1984), 229.

9)   See John Kenneth Galbraith, *Money: Whence it came, where it went*

(London: Penguin Books, 1989), 151.

10)   See Robert Triffin, *El caos monetario* (Mexico, DF: Fondo de Cultura Económica), 2; Milton Friedman and Anna Jacobson Schwartz, *A Monetary History of the United States 1867–1960* (Princeton: Princeton University Press, 1964), 199; Alan Greenspan, *La era de las turbulencias*, ed. B (Barcelona: S.A., 2008), 541.

11)   Louis W. Pauly, *The League of Nations and the Foreshadowing of the International Monetary Fund* (New Jersey: Princeton University, 1996), 7–11; Barry Eichengreen, *International Policy Coordination in Historical Perspective: A View from the Interwar Years* (Cambridge: National Bureau of Economic Research, 1984), 19; Manuel Várela Parache: *El oro en el sistema de Bretton Woods* (Madrid: Universidad Complutense de Madrid), 87, http://www.cepc.es; Lawrence H. Officer, "Gold Standard," in *EH.Net Encyclopaedia*, ed. Robert Whaples (Chicago: University of Illinois, 2008), 16.

12)   John Maynard Keynes, *Essays in Persuasion* (New York: Harcourt, Brace, and Company, 1932), 211–212.

13)   Ibid., 289.

14)   See Ian Shannon, *International Liquidity* (Melbourne: F. W. Cheshire Pty Ltd, 1964), 26.

15)   See Franklin D. Roosevelt, "Executive Order 6102—Requiring Gold Coin, Gold Bullion and Gold Certificates to Be Delivered to the Government," April 5, 1933, in *The American Presidency Project*, ed. Gerhard Peters and John T. Wooley, http://www.presidency.ucsb.edu/ws/?pid=14611. Milton Friedman and Anna Jacobson Schwartz, *A Monetary History of the United States 1867–1960* (Princeton: Princeton University Press, 1964), 463, 465, and 469.

16)   Franklin D. Roosevelt, *Fireside Chats* (Franklin D. Roosevelt Library and Museum, October 22, 1933).

17)   See Gary Richardson, Alejandro Komai, and Michael Gou, *Gold Reserve Act of 1934* (Washington: Federal Reserve, 2013); Milton Friedman and Anna Jacobson Schwartz, *A Monetary History of the United States 1867–1960* (Princeton: Princeton University Press, 1964), 465-471.

18)   See Ian Shannon, International Liquidity (Melbourne: F. W. Cheshire Pty Ltd, 1964), 32.

19)   V. Anikin, *The Yellow Devil* (Moscow: Progress Publishers, 1983), 71.

Francisco Soberón

An American economist, winner of the Economy Nobel Prize in 1990, wrote, "I can still recall the shock and incredulity of my Belgian colleagues at the University of Leuven in 1966 on learning that I, as an American citizen, could not then legally own monetary gold." Merton H. Miller, *Financial Innovations and Market Volatility* (Oxford: Blackwell, 1991), 3.

20)   *"In the turbulent interwar years, competitive devaluations in the wake of the demise of the gold-exchange standard presented policymakers in all countries with the dilemma of how to return to fixed exchange rates. The Tripartite Agreement, where Britain, France and the U.S. stabilized their exchange rates, represented a major achievement. The French had initially proposed a system where the franc, the dollar and sterling would fluctuate within narrow bounds. The three countries would agree not to devalue except by mutual consent and would coordinate support for the bilateral rates, with the eventual aim of restoring gold convertibility. However, American intransigence forced the French to drop fixed parities and the promise of a return to gold. The joint declaration known as the Tripartite Agreement issued by Washington, London and Paris simply affirmed the desire of the three countries to cooperate in minimizing exchange rate fluctuations and their commitment to free trade. For three years the nations exchange stabilization funds successfully reduced currency fluctuations."* Michael David Bordo et al., *An Overplayed Hand: France and the Bretton Woods International Monetary System* (New Brunswick, NJ: Rutgers University, 1994), 8.

21)   As explained by the Bank of England, in Great Britain the exchange control regulations established during World War II were very far reaching. *"The exchange control imposed during the 1939–45 War was wide ranging in its influence: it affected the foreign assets of people living in this country; the sterling assets of those living outside the sterling area; and all monetary transactions between the United Kingdom and countries outside the sterling area…In addition to their holdings of specified currencies, mentioned earlier, residents were required to offer for sale to the Treasury any gold bullion or gold coin in their possession. The London gold market during the war was allowed merely to collect and sell this gold to the Bank, or to buy from the Bank and sell to the trade gold needed for industrial purposes or for export in manufactured form. Dealings in foreign exchange during the war were limited to 'authorized dealers'—who had to deal, in most currencies, at published official rates of exchange and to cover transactions with the Bank at the same rate—charging their customers a commission. Virtually all of the foreign exchange broking firms ceased to function; and in many cases their partners and staff were recruited by the Bank for work on exchange control."* The U.K. Exchange Control: A Short History, The Bank of England, London, http://www.bankofengland.co.uk/archive/Documents/historicpubs/qb/1967/qb67q3245260.pdf.

CHAPTER 3

The Postwar Monetary System: The Initial Discussions

In the early years of World War II, the British Government asked John Maynard Keynes, to prepare a plan for a postwar monetary system. In the United States, experts of the Treasury Department were also working with a similar purpose. The main object of these tasks at that time was to answer proposals of the German minister of finance for a postwar financial system dominated by Germany. By 1943 Great Britain and the United States made their projects on this subject public. Since the beginning of the discussion of the different views about these projects, it was very clear that the United States had the power and the will to dictate the terms of any agreement that could eventually be reached. Under the prevailing scenario, there was no serious contender to replace the United States in these discussions. France was occupied and had a government in exile. Germany and Italy were enemy nations, so they took no part in the debates, and Great Britain—which was the only nation with certain influence, as it had not been invaded and was considered to have the most important economist at that time—fully depended on the material supply and financial support of the United States for its war efforts. In summary, Europe could not seriously oppose US ideas about the design of the postwar monetary system.

In the preliminary meeting to coordinate the future actions about this matter, the two main propositions discussed were the *Proposals for an International Clearing Union* formulated by Keynes and the

Francisco Soberón

Proposal for an International Stabilization Fund of the United and Associated Nations prepared by Harry Dexter White, assistant to the secretary of the Treasury Department of the United States. Keynes's proposal had been circulated within the British Treasury on September 8, 1941. Ministers received a fourth draft on February 11, 1942, and the British government issued the final draft in April 1943.

As regards White's proposal, its first definitive version was a mimeographed draft dated April 1942. The US Treasury issued the final version in printed form on July 10, 1943.[1]

In very brief terms, Keynes proposed to establish an International Clearing Union (ICU) based on international bank-money, called *bancor*, fixed (but not unalterably) in terms of gold and accepted as the equivalent of gold by all the members of this organization for the purpose of settling international balances. The central banks of all member states would keep accounts with the ICU, through which they would be entitled to settle their exchange balances with one another at their par value as defined in terms of *bancor*. Countries having a favorable balance of payments with the rest of the world as a whole would find themselves in possession of a credit account with the ICU, and those having an unfavorable balance would have a debit account. Measures would be established to prevent the piling up of credit and debit balances without limit, since the system would fail in the long run if it did not possess sufficient capacity for self-equilibrium to secure this. Keynes explained that the idea underlying such a union was to generalize the essential principle of banking as within any closed system: the principle of the necessary equality of credits and debits.

According to Keynes's proposal, the member states should agree among themselves on the initial values of their own currencies in terms of *bancor*, and the governing board of the ICU should fix the value of *bancor* in terms of gold. Each member state should be assigned a *quota*, which should determine the measure of its responsibility in the management of the ICU and of its right to enjoy the credit facilities provided by the union. The initial quotas would be fixed by reference to the average sum of each country's exports and imports during the three prewar years.

Keynes suggested that member states should adopt measures to avoid any persistent credit or debit balance by any member with the ICU, including the depreciation or appreciation of its local currency in terms of *bancor* within certain limits, as might be necessary.

Keynes emphasized that the analogy of his plan with a national banking system was complete, as no depositor in a local bank suffers because the balances, which the depositor leaves idle, are employed to finance the business of someone else. The substitution of a credit mechanism in place of hoarding would repeat in the international field the same miracle, already performed in the domestic field, of "turning a stone into bread."

Keynes underlined that his provision differed in one important respect from the prewar system; he aimed at putting some part of the responsibility for adjustment on the creditor country as well as on the debtor, since he thought that the creditor should not be allowed to remain entirely passive. For if it was, an intolerably heavy task might be laid on the debtor country, which for that very reason would already be in the weaker position.

Regarding the position of gold within the monetary order he pointed out that gold still possessed great psychological value and the desire to possess a gold reserve against unforeseen contingencies was likely to remain. He accepted that gold also had the merit of providing an uncontroversial standard of value for international purposes, for which it would not yet be easy to find a serviceable substitute.

He made a very important point to avoid confrontation with the United States, as he explained that it was not reasonable to ask the United States to demonetize the stock of gold that formed the basis of its impregnable liquidity. He left the door open regarding future alternatives about this question by saying that what, in the long run, the world might decide to do with gold was another matter. He clarified that the purpose of the ICU was to supplant gold as a governing factor, not to dispense with it.

Under the terms of his plan, the international *bancor* would be defined in terms of a weight of gold, and since the national currencies of the member states would have a defined exchange value in terms of *bancor*, it followed that they would each have a defined gold content, which would be their official buying price for gold.

Concerning the question of the exchange control regulations, he considered that no country could safely allow the flight of funds for political reasons, to evade domestic taxation, or in anticipation of the owner turning refugee. Equally, no country could safely receive fugitive funds, which constitute an unwanted import of capital yet could not safely be used for fixed investment. For these reasons he held that control of capital movements, both inward and outward, should be a permanent feature of the postwar system. The specific situation of Great Britain clearly influenced his position. India and some other countries of the sterling area were holding large amounts of sterling, and they wanted to be able to use these balances, without any restriction, to make payments in any market. Great Britain considered this unacceptable, since it did not have the foreign-exchange reserves that would be necessary to support such arrangements. Related to this question, Keynes pointed out that the position of abnormal balances in overseas ownership held in various countries at the end of the war presented a problem of considerable importance and special difficulty.

The early versions of Keynes's proposal contained a stipulation by which he claimed that, in view of Great Britain's experience and geographical and political position in relation to Europe and the United States, the head office of the ICU should be situated in London, with the board of managers meeting alternately there and in Washington. The draft finally published in 1943 did not include this suggestion.

Finally, the ambitious nature of Keynes's plan was clearly shown, as he underlined that the ICU might become the pivot of the future economic government of the world.[2]

In summary, the Keynes Plan would have established a system that would provide liquidity automatically—something extremely important to Great Britain under the dominant circumstances at that time—and achieve the goal of an equilibrium in the balance of payments and the stability in rates of exchange that had prevailed during the gold-standard periods, while distributing the responsibilities of maintaining these targets between debtors and creditors and using a banking currency universally accepted: the *bancor*.

White's plan, on the other hand, provided for the creation of an International Stabilization Fund of the United and Associated Nations (ISF) as a permanent institution for international monetary cooperation. The creation of this organization was finally agreed on at the Bretton Woods Conference, under the name of the International Monetary Fund.

White's proposal established that the resources of the ISF would be available under adequate safeguards to maintain currency stability, while giving member countries time to correct maladjustments in their balance of payments without resorting to extreme measures destructive of international prosperity.

White clarified that the resources of the ISF would not be used to prolong a basically unbalanced international position. On the contrary, the fund had to be influential in inducing countries to pursue policies making for an orderly return to equilibrium.

White's proposal outlined the following purposes of the ISF:

1. To help stabilize the foreign-exchange rates of the currencies of the United Nations and the countries associated with them.

2. To shorten the periods and lessen the degree of disequilibrium in the international balance of payments of member countries.

3. To help create conditions that foster the smooth flow of foreign trade and of productive capital among the member countries.

4. To facilitate the effective utilization of the blocked foreign

balances accumulating in some countries as a consequence of the war situation.

5. To reduce the use of such foreign-exchange restrictions, bilateral clearing arrangements, multiple currency devices, and discriminatory foreign-exchange practices as hamper world trade and the international flow of productive capital.

Each of the member countries of the ISF had to subscribe to a specified quota, a part of which had to be paid in gold. White proposed that the quota for each member country should be computed by a formula that gave due weight to the important relevant factors (e. g. a country's holdings of gold and free foreign exchange, the magnitude and the fluctuations of its balance of international payments, its national income, etc.). This was one of the most complicated subjects of his plan, and I will revert to this question in the pages that follow.

White proposed a monetary unit of the ISF, to be called *unitas*, equal in value to 137 1/7 grains of fine gold (equivalent to ten dollars). No change in the gold value of the *unitas* could be made except with the approval of 85 percent of the member votes. The value of the currency of each member country should be established in terms of *unitas*. For any country that became a member prior to the date on which the ISF operations would begin, the rates initially used should be based upon the value of the currency in terms of US dollars that prevailed on July 1, 1943. The ISF would have the faculty to determine the range within which the rates of exchange of member currencies would be permitted to fluctuate. Changes in the exchange value of the currency of a member country should be considered only when essential to the correction of fundamental disequilibrium in its balance of payments, and they should be made only with the approval of three-fourths of the member votes, including the representative of the country concerned. The United States had the responsibility of keeping the dollar price of gold fixed at thirty-five dollars per troy ounce. This implied that it had to adjust the supply of dollars to maintain confidence in its future gold convertibility.

Each member country of the fund would undertake the following:

1. To maintain by appropriate action exchange rates established by the fund for the currencies of other countries, and not to alter exchange rates except as provided, although exchange rates of member countries may be permitted to fluctuate within the specified range fixed by the fund.

2. Not to engage in exchange dealings with member or nonmember countries that would undermine stability of exchange rates established by the fund.

3. To abandon, as soon as the member country decided that conditions permitted, all restrictions (other than those involving capital transfers) over foreign-exchange transactions with other member countries, and not to impose any additional restrictions (except upon capital transfers) without the approval of the fund.

White's proposal also included the creation of an International Bank for Reconstruction and Development, which would be responsible for providing financial assistance for economic development and the reconstruction after World War II.[3]

Summarizing, White proposed to organize a monetary system with the dollar substituting for gold as the center, with fixed exchange rates, and to create a supranational organization clearly under the control of the United States, which would be in charge of the system.

Experts who have studied both plans consider that "they reflected the different economic situations of the two countries, and hence their contrasting interests. Britain was heavily in debt to the USA, and the Keynes Plan, therefore, was attentive to the interests of international debtors. The USA was the world's largest creditor, and had every expectation of continuing to run large current account surpluses after the war. Consequently, the White Plan reflected the USA's unwillingness as creditor to carry all of the burdens of restoring an open, multilateral system of payments. It proposed a much smaller provision of international liquidity than the Keynes Plan, and stronger mechanisms to induce debtors to make adjustments to bring their balances of payments into equilibrium."[4]

In very few words, Keynes was looking for a countervailing balance to the United States, an *International Clearing Union* that would function as a world central bank, issue a world currency (the *bancor*), and regulate the flow of credit. White just wanted to create an agency that would preserve the central role of the US dollar in international finance.

In addition to White's and Keynes's proposals, there were also documents containing French and Canadian plans. The French plan was written by André Istel, adviser to the French government and a negotiator of the Franco-British agreement of 1939, who would become a delegate at Bretton Woods, and Hervé Alphand, the former French financial attaché in Washington, who worked for General de Gaulle on financial and economic issues. The French Plan, *Suggestions Regarding International Monetary Relations*, was not considered an official plan, although it had the personal support of General de Gaulle. Under the French Plan, the participants would have fixed their official parities in terms of the currencies of the other participants, and these parities would change only after consultation. The parities would be maintained by intervention of each member transacting with the monetary authorities of the other members. Each member would hold other members' currencies, to increase liquidity, up to limits. To protect the members from exchange risk, collateral (in the form of gold, foreign bills, raw materials, approved securities, etc.) would have been required for any national currency held by the monetary authorities of another participating country. The plan suggested a monetary stabilization office as a possible mechanism to facilitate clearings and to serve as a depository for the collateral. The French considered the plan they proposed as a first step toward a general return to an international gold standard.[5]

The Canadian plan was a sort of compromise between the Keynes and White proposals. Its author was Louis Rasminsky, who later on was a delegate at Bretton Woods. Regarding these two plans, it is clear that they were never seriously taken into consideration, and the experts that participated in the Bretton Woods Conference and its previous meeting pointed out that they had no time to debate more than two plans and that there were few instances in which countries other than the United States and Great Britain would be able to influence the final outcome.

American and British delegations of experts, led by White and Keynes respectively, met to discuss the American and British proposals in April 1944.

During these meetings, the experts concentrated on whether it was desirable to establish an international currency (*bancor* in Keynes's Plan and *unitas* in White's Plan). Once Keynes realized that his plan had no chance to go ahead, he wanted to raise *unitas* to the status of an international currency, while White argued that Keynes was trying to press for his ICU proposal with another name. Finally the experts abandoned the idea of an international currency and agreed to establish a par value system, in which the value of any currency should be fixed in terms of dollars, and the dollar should be fixed in terms of gold at a price of thirty-five dollars per troy ounce Some experts consider it paradoxical that the adoption of an international unit of account was discarded in the course of the Anglo-American negotiations, taking into account that the British and the US representatives agreed on the opportunity of introducing an international unit of account in their respective original plans.

A possible answer may perhaps be sought for in the different roles assigned to the international unit of account in the two schemes. As Horsefield has pointed out: "for Keynes this would have been a true medium of exchange...for White it was no more than a standard of value." This is usually understood as a further confirmation of Keynes's alleged inflationary spur, as opposed to sound principles of orthodox finance. According to this interpretation, the Keynes plan provided for the creation ex nihilo of a new international medium of exchange, whereas the White plan remained soundly anchored to the available quantity of the old international medium of exchange, i.e. gold.[6]

As a result of these meetings, the United States and other Allied countries agreed to and simultaneously published a *Joint Statement* on April 21, 1944. Such *Joint Statement* reflected the terms of White's proposals. It was clear that the United States had imposed its terms, and Great Britain had had no alternative but to accept its conditions, since it was totally dependent on American supply and finance to support its war effort.

In May 1944, the United States invited most of the world's independent countries (excluding, of course, its war enemies) to an international monetary conference to be held in Bretton Woods.

The United States also invited a smaller group of countries to a preliminary conference in Atlantic City, New Jersey, to work out a draft proposal for the Bretton Woods conference. This meeting, held from June 15–30, 1944, produced a series of alternatives to provisions in the *Joint Statement* that, with the *Joint Statement* itself, formed the basis of discussion on the IMF at Bretton Woods.[7]

The Bretton Woods Conference

The International Monetary and Financial Conference of the United and Associated Nations—the official name of the Bretton Woods Conference—finally took place at the Mount Washington Hotel in Bretton Woods, New Hampshire, from July 1 to July 22, 1944.[8]

Everybody understood that the United States had complete control of the situation and that the European countries could not put up much resistance to American positions.

As has already been mentioned, Europe was devastated and its economy in ruins because of the crisis of the 1930s, followed by five years of war. They were indebted to the United States and fully dependent on this country for the final success of their war efforts. The US economy was strong due to the high demand from their allies during the years of war. They had become the world creditors, and they held 70 percent of the world's gold reserves. Their reserves in 1945 were 17,848 metric tons of gold. In contrast, the European countries with the highest reserves were Great Britain, with 1,773 metric tons, and France, with 1,378 metric tons.[9] In summary, the United States had become the hegemonic power of the world, and Europe had no alternative but to surrender to its power.[10]

Moreover, the conference was held the month after the disembarkation of American troops in Normandy, which definitely increased the military and political influence of the United States.

Under these circumstances, there was no doubt that everything in the conference would go according to the American plans and that its predictable outcome would be the approval of the White proposals with only those modifications that the Americans felt did not affect their interests. Moreover, the US was completely in charge of the preparation, staffing and organization of the conference. The US technical staff numbered thirty-three—by far the largest staff at the conference. And unlike those from any other country, five members of the US technical team were active conference participants. If that wasn't enough, the thirty-nine members of the conference secretariat were all Americans.

The conference was divided into three commissions. White chaired Commission I, which dealt with the most important subject— organization of the International Stabilization Fund, which was the entity that would be in charge of the international monetary system and the main aspects of its future functioning. Keynes was relegated to chair Commission II, which was responsible for the organization of the International Bank for Reconstruction and Development.[11] There was also a Commission III, with such an abstract inauspicious denomination as *other means of international cooperation*, chaired by a Mexican expert.

The lesser importance of Commissions II and III is widely accepted. The editors of the transcripts of the conference, which have already been mentioned in this book, acknowledge that Commission III was a venue for ideas that did not fall under the other two commissions, it held fewer meetings, and "its recommendations left no lasting impact" because the commission neither established a new international organization nor significantly changed any existing organization. They also point out that the coverage of the transcripts was extensive "for Commission I but contain less material on Commissions II and III because 'they were lower priorities for the conference' and received less coverage from the pool of stenographers."[12]

The way the conference was conducted left no doubt that the United States worked in every detail to impose those conditions that fit their national interests in all respects. This is clearly acknowledged by American experts who attended the conference, such as Raymond F. Mikesell, who was at that time an economist in the Division of Monetary Research in the Treasury Department. Says Professor Mikesell:

Bretton Woods was a drafting meeting, with the substance having been largely settled beforehand by the U.S. and U.K. delegations and supported by the Canadians. The drafting process was skilfully guided and executed by American technicians, who served, either as members of the Secretariat to the conference or as advisors to the U.S. delegation. In practice, it did not matter which hat they wore. Although delegates from other countries made numerous proposals that conflicted with the basic preconference position and agenda, the technicians were positioned to prevent their introduction into the charters. The commissions and committees at Bretton Woods presented a facade of democratic procedure, but the outcome had been largely predetermined by the U.S. and U.K. delegations."[13]

Furthermore, other experts who have studied in detail the work of the conference emphasize that "whether the delegates were aware of it or not the important decisions were made behind closed doors between the American delegation and the foreign delegation involved. While Harry White and his small group of technical advisers kept absolute control over the text of the articles to be included in the agreement, the powerhouse of the conference was in Morgenthau's office (Secretary of the Treasury Department of the United States), where some of the most difficult and troublesome issues had to be settled."[14]

All above information confirms the idea that there was little room for any serious debate at the Bretton Woods Conference and that its outcome had already been determined by the government of the United States before its commencement. Nevertheless, the aspect that gives the clearest idea about how things were worked out at that meeting was the question referred to as one of its more important points: the distribution of the quotas that would define the voting powers of the members and would therefore reflect their final and real influence in the decision-making procedures of the *International Stabilization Fund* (ISF—which by the time of the Bretton Woods meeting had already been renamed the International Monetary Fund (IMF). This was supposed to be the organization that would be in charge of the management of the new international monetary system.

For this purpose, nothing is better than to refer to the testimony of the already mentioned Professor Mikesell:

In mid-April 1943 shortly after the White Plan was made public, White called me to his office and asked that I prepare a formula for the ISF quotas that would be based on the member's gold and dollars holdings, national incomes, and foreign trade. He gave no instructions on the weights to be used, but I was to give the United States a quota of approximately $2.9 billion; the United Kingdom (including its colonies), about half the U.S. quota; the Soviet Union, an amount just under that of the United Kingdom; and China, somewhat less. He also wanted the total of the quotas to be about $10 billion. White's major concern was that our military allies (President Roosevelt's big four) should have the largest quotas, with a ranking on which the president *and the secretary of state had agreed. I was surprised that White did not mention France, which was usually regarded as being third in economic importance among the Allied powers. He said that he did not care where France ranked, and its ranking did not need to be an objective in the exercise. As was typical, White wanted something on his desk in a couple of days— it took me four, including a weekend. A modern computer would have saved several days of work on my state-of-the-art calculator and might have produced a more credible result.* [15]

With this background in mind, it is not surprising that when the information about the quotas assigned to each country was put forward in Commission I, many delegations were upset and reacted very strongly regarding the specific quotas assigned to their countries. According to Professor Mikesell, White instructed him not to reveal the formula that had been used to determine the quotas. Such instruction could be understood, since the formula to calculate the quotas was actually designed—as per the testimony of its author already quoted— to benefit the main allies of the United States following the express instructions of the president of the country and, in general, to suit American political interests. More than half the delegates strongly objected, and several demanded to know how the quotas had been calculated.

Professor Mikesell gave a seminar on the factors taken into account in calculating the quotas, but he did not reveal the formula used. According to his own words, "I tried to make the process appear as scientific as possible, but the delegates were intelligent enough to know that the process was more political than scientific." [16]

In the case of the French delegation, the protest was particularly strong. They expressed their great disappointment about the fact that the quota assigned to France did not meet their expectations. They said that the idea discussed in previous consultations regarding this subject was to establish quotas on the basis of mathematical arguments, which they had supposed would be readily accepted by public opinion.

However, a possible agreement on this basis found difficulties, and it came to negotiations among different nations, and several nations saw their quotas increased while others saw theirs diminished. The French delegation added that the negotiations had resulted in a great deal of confusion, which they objected to. They emphasized that the influence attributed toward Europe, and especially to Western Europe and France, did not seem to amount to its just value. They asked to send back to the Quota Committee the proposed figures for reconsideration, and they threatened to reconsider French participation in the fund if the question of quotas could not be reevaluated.[17] As could be envisaged, the American proposition was finally approved, with the reservations of Australia, India, Iran, and France. The protest of the latter country continued after the official meeting, and Professor Mikesell acknowledged in his memoirs that "the French delegation represented the de Gaulle government in exile, and it was well known that President Roosevelt and the U.S. Administration were not on good terms with de Gaulle. I believe that Mendes-France (chairman of the French delegation and years later Prime Minister of France) regarded the decision on the French quota as a deliberate insult."[18]

The distribution of the quotas clearly revealed the degree of the control that the United States exercised at the Conference—and already in world affairs in general. In 1947 its quota was about one-third of the total, and put together with that of its most loyal ally, Great Britain, they represented almost half of the total. Latin America and the Caribbean had in total about eight percent, and the only three African countries that participated in the conference had around two percent combined.[19]

The predictable outcome of the Bretton Woods Conference was the adoption of the Articles of Agreement of the International Monetary Fund (IMF) and the International Bank for Reconstruction and Development (known as World Bank), along the main lines proposed by the American delegation to the Conference, which as already mentioned had previously been conciliated with the British delegation.

As a matter of fact, it was agreed that principal offices of both organizations should be located "in the territory of the member having the largest quota" and that "at least one-half of the holdings of the Fund shall be held in the depository designated by the member in whose territories the IMF has its principal office," a complicated way of saying that the headquarters of the fund and its money should be in the United States.

As regards Great Britain, its acceptance of the American positions was subject to a bilateral agreement by which the United States agreed to make available substantial bilateral financial assistance. Under this agreement, the United States opened a credit line to Great Britain for 3.75 billion dollars and 650 million to cover other British war liabilities.[20]

As far as France was concerned, the humiliation that the United States inflicted on this country, by assigning a quota that was clearly below its political and economic importance, had very far reaching consequences. No doubt, it was among the causes of the bitter criticism of President de Gaulle to the *exorbitant privileges* of the dollar under the Bretton Woods system and his policy to continuously exchange for gold the dollars that France was accumulating due to its balance of payments surplus in the sixties.

The Soviet Union did not ratify the agreement, and in 1947 it assumed a very critical view about the Bretton Woods institutions, calling them "branches of Wall Street."

The Articles of Agreement of the IMF: The Right of the Strongest

In *The Social Contract*, Jean-Jacques Rousseau said, "The strongest is never strong enough to be always the master unless he transforms strength into right, and obedience into duty."[21] To a great extent, this can be applied to the terms of the IMF Articles of Agreement (AA), which transformed into a legal document the conditions of a monetary system conceived to suit the interests of the strongest country: the United States.

In the first place, the elimination of the concept of an international currency consolidated the dollar's position as the center of the international monetary system. As the par value of the currency of each member should be expressed in terms of gold as a common denominator or in terms of the dollar, it followed that countries would maintain their international reserves mainly in gold and dollars, which meant additional economic influence and a cheap source of finance, as already mentioned.

In the second place, the Keynes Plan would have created liquidity of *bancor* amounting to about thirty billion dollars. This liquidity would have been automatically available to the members of the *International Clearing Union*. In other words, a member would not have required any specific authorization to use its quota of *bancor*. It is easy to understand that this was not acceptable to the United States, since this could weaken its very strong position as the main creditor of the world. On the contrary, the AA just allowed any member to borrow from the IMF by swapping the national currencies deposited there *under adequate safeguards*. Moreover, the total funds that the IMF would have according to the agreed quotas were less than one-third of the estimated amount of liquidity as per Keynes's proposal. If the IMF was of the opinion that any member was using such resources in a manner contrary to its purposes, it might limit the use of its resources by the member and might even declare that member ineligible to use its resources. Therefore, funds were not automatically at the disposal of any member that required them, and the IMF could definitely exercise its discretion when deciding about this question. Considering the voting power of the United States, it is clear that any final decision on this subject had to come with its previous endorsement.[22]

In the third place, one of the express purposes of the IMF was to assist in the elimination of foreign-exchange restrictions. The articles also established that no member might exercise exchange control in a manner that would restrict payments for current transactions, so no member could impose any restriction on the making of payments and transfers for current international transactions without the approval of the IMF. Summarizing, the IMF established strict regulations regarding the international flow of capital and was in charge of ensuring that every country abided by them, which conferred great power to this organization in international financial relations.[23]

And, in the fourth place, the articles established that a member could not propose a change in the par value of its currency, except to correct a *fundamental disequilibrium*, and such change could be made only after consultation with the IMF. No definition of the exact meaning of *fundamental disequilibrium* is contained in the AA or in any other related document, so the IMF could exercise a great deal of discretion when deciding whether any request of a member was appropriate. If a country changed the par value of its currency despite the objection of the IMF, it could be declared ineligible to use the resources of the IMF, and it could even be required to withdraw from membership. As the United States had a majority of the voting powers of this organization, this actually meant that all member countries were subject to the approval of the US government in making any change in the par value of their respective currencies. It goes without saying that the United States would not accept any change in the par value of the currencies that could weaken the international position of the dollar and its political and economic interests.[24]

In summary, the structure of the IMF and the terms of its AA meant that from there on the United States could control the rates of exchange of any member country and have the final word about IMF lending policy. The United States would also have a decisive influence on international exchange control regulations, and the articles consolidated the position of the dollar as the world's principal reserve currency and medium of exchange. Furthermore, the IMF would be based in Washington, and most of its resources would be deposited in American territory. Probably there are not many instances of an international conference where one of its participants obtained so many vital prerogatives.

But notwithstanding the great success of the United States in the Bretton Woods Conference, the system agreed had in itself the seed of a contradiction that could finally make it collapse. As pointed out by the American economist Robert Triffin while testifying before the Congress of the United States in 1960, there was a fundamental problem in the international monetary system agreed upon in Bretton Woods:

If the United States stopped running balance of payments deficits, the international community would lose its largest source of additions to reserves. The resulting shortage of liquidity could pull the world economy into a contractionary spiral, leading to instability, whereas if U.S. deficits continued, a steady stream of dollars would continue to fuel world economic growth. However, excessive U.S. deficits (dollar glut) would erode confidence in the value of the U.S. dollar. Without confidence in the dollar, it would no longer be accepted as the world's reserve currency. The fixed exchange rate system could break down, leading to instability.[25]

As can be seen in the next chapter, the United States did not correct the deficits of the balance of payments; it ran out of gold to redeem its dollars, and this generated the suspension of dollar convertibility and the final collapse of the Bretton Woods system.

Francisco Soberón

Notes and Bibliography

1)   See J. Keith Horsefield, *The International Monetary Fund, 20 years of International Monetary Cooperation*, Volume III: Documents (Washington: IMF), 3, 37.

2)   See Ibid., 21–22, 27–28, 30, 32.

3)   See Ibid., 85, 87, 95.

4)   Douglas J. Forsyth, *"Restoring International Payments: Germany and France Confront Bretton Woods and the European Payments Union"* (working paper 1997/111, Ohio, December 1997), 2.

5)   See Michael Bordo et al., *An Overplayed Hand: France and the Bretton Woods International Monetary System* (New Brunswick, NJ: Rutgers University, 1994), 5.

6)   Massimo Amato and Luca Fantacci, *Back to which Bretton Woods? Liquidity and clearing as alternative principles for reforming international finance* (Milano: Bocconi University, 2009), 5.

7)   See Kurt Schuler and Andrew Rosenberg, *The Bretton Woods Transcripts* (Washington: Center for Financial Stability, 2013), 4–5.

8)   *"The International Monetary and Financial Conference of the United and Associated Nations, as it was officially called, took place at the Mount Washington Hotel in Bretton Woods, New Hampshire, from July 1 to July 22, 1944. There were several reasons for choosing Bretton Woods as the location of the conference. The summer climate was temperate, a key consideration because air conditioning was not yet widespread. ('For God's sake do not take us to Washington in July, which would surely be a most unfriendly act,' Keynes had written to White in May 1944.) The remote location offered greater security and seclusion than would have been possible in a large city. Unlike many other resort hotels of the time, the Mount Washington Hotel accepted Jews as guests, and many staff and delegates at the conference were Jews. Finally, the Democratic administration of President Franklin Roosevelt sought bipartisan support for any agreement that would arise from the conference. Senator Charles Tobey of New Hampshire was the senior Republican on the Senate Committee on Banking and Currency, whose approval would be vital for the agreement. Tobey, who was facing an opponent in the Republican primary election, suggested holding the conference in New Hampshire as a way of showing the people of his state that he was influential. The Roosevelt administration accepted Tobey's suggestion as a way of winning his favour for the*

agreement. Originally the conference was scheduled to end on July 19, but it was extended for a few days to complete its work. Delegates from 44 nations plus a representative of Denmark and observers from several international organizations attended." Schuler and Rosenberg, *The Bretton Woods Transcripts, 4.*

9) World Gold Council, *Historical Statistics.*

10) In the nineties, the minister of foreign relations of an important Western European country told me with a clear frustrated feeling, "The fact that European countries used the first half of the twentieth century to fight against each other while the United States used it to enrich itself, has been extremely costly to us."

11) *"The outstanding personality at Bretton Woods was Lord Keynes. He shone in two respects—in the fact that he is, of course, one of the brightest lights of mankind in both thinking and expression, and in his ability to influence people, and he shone also by being the world's worst chairman. He presided over meetings of the Bank in a way that was entirely intolerable because he had his own documents all fixed up so that he could go through in a hurry. He spoke while he was sitting down in a meeting and it was difficult to hear him. He spoke indistinctly when presiding and was impatient of any difference of opinion."* Armand Van Dormael, *The Bretton Woods Conference: Birth of a Monetary System* (California: Hoover Institution, Stanford University, 1978), 8–9.

12) See Schuler and Rosenberg, *The Bretton Woods Transcripts*, XVI, 10, 13.

13) Raymond F. Mikesell, *The Bretton Woods Debates: A Memoir* (Princeton: Department of Economics, Princeton University, 1994), 34.

14) Van Dormael, *The Bretton Woods Conference*, 14.

15) Mikesell, *The Bretton Woods Debates*, 22.

16) Ibid., 36.

17) See Schuler and Rosenberg, *The Bretton Woods Transcripts*, 66–67.

18) Mikesell, *The Bretton Woods Debates*, 37.

19) See Eric Toussaint, *The Creation of the Bretton Woods Institutions* (Liège: CADTM, 2006).

20) Robert Triffin, *El caos monetario* (Mexico: Fondo de Cultura Económica, 1961), 136–137.

21) *The Social Contract*, Jean-Jacques Rousseau, 2, http://www. earlymoderntexts. com/assets/ pdfs/rousseau1762.pdf.

22)   See *Articles of Agreement of the International Monetary Fund*, July 22, 1944, Article V. Section 5, and Article I. point v.

23)   See Ibid., Article I. point IV, Article VI. Section 3, and Article VIII. Section 2.

Considering the specific situation of Great Britain at the time regarding the large sterling holdings of India and other countries of the sterling area, (already mentioned in this book) and the very difficult economic conditions of other European nations, the following provision was included in the AA: *"In the post-war transitional period members may, notwithstanding the provisions of any other articles of this Agreement, maintain restrictions on payments and transfers for current international transactions... members shall withdraw restrictions maintained or imposed under this Section as soon as they are satisfied that they will be able, in the absence of such restrictions, to settle their balance of payments in a manner which will not unduly encumber their access to the resources of the Fund."* Ibid., Article XIV. Section 2.

24)   See Ibid., Article IV and Article XV.

25)   *Money Matters, System in Crisis 1959–1971*, Part 4 (Washington: International Monetary Fund).

CHAPTER 4

The Crisis of the Postwar Monetary System: The Gold Drain

In the years that followed the end of World War II, Europe was completely devastated. Probably there is no better description of its situation than the one given by the then secretary of state of the United States, George Marshall, in 1947. Said Mr. Marshall:

In considering the requirements for the rehabilitation of Europe, the physical loss of life, the visible destruction of cities, factories, mines and railroads was correctly estimated but it has become obvious during recent months that this visible destruction was probably less serious than the dislocation of the entire fabric of European economy. For the past 10 years conditions have been highly abnormal. The feverish preparation for war and the more feverish maintenance of the war effort engulfed all aspects of national economies. Machinery has fallen into disrepair or is entirely obsolete. Under the arbitrary and destructive Nazi rule, virtually every possible enterprise was geared into the German war machine. Long-standing commercial ties, private institutions, banks, insurance companies, and shipping companies disappeared, through loss of capital, absorption through nationalization, or by simple destruction. In many countries, confidence in the local currency has been severely shaken. The breakdown of the business structure of Europe during the war was complete.[1]

In 1947 European lost about one-third of its reserves of gold and dollars to finance the deficit of its balance of payments.[2] The resources available in the Word Bank were clearly not enough to finance Europe's reconstruction, while the IMF, according to its purpose, was only lending to cover balance-of-payments deficits. As a palliative to this situation, the Americans arranged for a bilateral assistance program—the Marshall Plan, which provided facilities for about thirteen billion dollars.

Under the prevailing circumstances, major European countries and Japan were unable to make their currencies freely convertible, and they used capital controls to maintain undervalued real exchange rates against the dollar in the pursuit of export-led growth.[3] Some of them resorted to large devaluations; for instance, in January 1948, France devalued the franc by 80 percent, and in September 1949, Great Britain devalued the pound by 30.5 percent. Nine other nations immediately followed: Australia, India, South Africa, New Zealand, Ireland, Denmark, Norway, Egypt, and Israel.[4]

In the following years, the United States continued to be the main creditor of the world. In the ten years from 1946 through 1955, the deficit of the world in its current account with the United States reached the amount of thirty-eight billion dollars.[5] Its gold reserves continuously grew, and in 1952 they reached the record amount of 20,663 metric tons, whereas that year Germany accumulated only 124 metric tons, and the reserves of Great Britain and France had decreased to 1,317 and 517 metric tons respectively.[6]

Meanwhile, European countries and Japan advanced in their reconstruction programs. Germany and Japan in particular, which faced restrictions in their arms expenditure, were using their resources to build new efficient industrial plants, whereas the United States—which came through the Second Word War with its prewar industrial plants intact and thus becoming comparatively obsolescent—was suffering from relatively inefficient production. As the dollar was maintained at a fixed rate of exchange with the currencies of European countries and Japan, those countries' products became more competitive than American ones. As a matter of fact, this new situation had a very positive impact on the balance of payments in Europe and

Japan. The goods and services account in the balance of payments of Europe changed from a deficit of about [7] billion in 1947 to growing surpluses (from 700 million to 1.8 billion) between 1952 and 1956. The United States' balance-of-payments position progressively weakened, and foreigners as a group were acquiring more dollars than they were spending. The scarcity of dollars experienced during the first postwar years transformed into the so-called "dollar glut," the gold reserves of the United States progressively declined, and European nations' holdings of dollars increased. The American gold reserves started to decrease steadily in 1957.[7]

In the sixties, this new economic and financial scenario was not due only to the surpluses in the balance of payments of the European countries. It was also linked to political factors. While the European territory was the theater of the two world wars in the first half of the twentieth century, the United States, several thousand miles away, was considered the safest place to keep deposits and gold holdings, and this attracted huge financial resources. However, in the sixties—in the middle of the Cold War and the Vietnam War—Switzerland and other European countries offered a serious alternative to those looking for the most convenient and safe place to keep their wealth.

In 1958, thirteen European countries made their currencies freely convertible into dollars and other currencies for nonresidents—a clear sign of their economic progress and increased credibility before the financial markets.

The surpluses in the balance of payments of the European countries meant a continuous increase in their dollar holdings, part of which they used to buy gold from the United States at the official price of thirty-five dollars per troy ounce. This policy was particularly active in the case of France, which, besides, maintained a very public policy to strongly criticize the prerogatives of the dollar under the Bretton Woods agreements.

In February 1965 General de Gaulle held a press conference in which he addressed in very frank and clear terms the problems of the

Francisco Soberón

international monetary system and, in particular, the privileges of the dollar under this regime. He referred to the reasons that were taken into consideration in 1944 to reach the agreement in which the dollar became the center of that system. He also explained how the situation was completely different twenty years later. Said General de Gaulle:

The currencies of Western nations have been rehabilitated, so much so that the total gold reserves of the Six are now equal to those of the United States. They would be even higher if the Six determined to convert all their dollar holdings into gold. It is therefore clear that the convention under which the dollar is an international currency of transcendent value no longer rests on the initial basis, which was that the United States owned the major part of the world's gold.

But there is more. The fact that many countries as a matter of principle accept dollars as well as gold to offset the U.S. balance of payments deficits leads to a situation wherein the United States is heavily in debt without having to pay. Indeed, what the United States owes to foreign countries it pays—at least in part—with dollars that it can simply issue if it chooses to. It does so instead of paying fully with gold whose value is real, which one owns only because one has earned it, and which cannot be transferred to other countries without any danger or any sacrifice. This unilateral facility that is available to the United States contributes to the gradual disappearance of the idea that the dollar is an impartial and international trade medium, whereas it is in fact a credit instrument reserved for one state only.

Actually such a situation carries other consequences. In particular, the United States is under no obligation to settle its payments deficits in gold—at least not for the full amount—as was the case formerly under the old rule, which required states to take adequate—and sometimes stringent—steps to correct their disequilibrium.

...huge amounts of money are created in the United States and subsequently exported overseas in the form of dollar loans extended to foreign countries or private individuals. In view of the fact that in the United States this generates an increase in the total credit proxy,

80

so that investments at home are less remunerative, there emerges in the United States an increasing propensity to invest overseas. Hence, in some countries, some sort of expropriation of a number of undertakings...

...circumstances today are such that one can even wonder how serious a disturbance there would be if all countries holding dollars came to request, sooner or later, conversion into gold. Even though such a widespread move may never come to pass, it is a fact that there is, so to speak, a fundamental disequilibrium.

To correct such problems, he proposed a return to the rules of the gold standard: "Yes, gold, which does not change in nature, which can be made either into bars, ingots, or coins, which has no nationality, which is considered, in all places and at all times, the immutable and fiduciary value par excellence."[8]

A day later, Jacques Rueff, one of the main economic advisers to General de Gaulle, went further and offered a very graphic and critical description regarding the way that the international monetary system agreed upon in Bretton Woods worked. In an interview with the *Economist* of London, Mr. Rueff explained that when a country with a *key currency*, such as the United States, had a balance-of-payments deficit, it paid the creditor country dollars, which ended up with the latter's central bank but were then re-lent to the New York money market, so they returned to the place of origin. He added that the debtor country did not lose what the creditor country had gained. So the key currency country never felt the effect of a deficit in its balance of payments. And the main consequence was that the country had no reason whatever to make the deficit disappear, because it did not appear. Mr. Rueff concluded, "Let me be more positive: If I had an agreement with my tailor that whatever money I pay him he returns to me the very same day as a loan, I would have no objection at all to ordering more suits from him and my own balance of payments would then be in deficit."[9]

No doubt, France's position was certainly influenced by the

humiliation suffered during the Bretton Woods Conference on the subject of the distribution of the quotas, and it was backed by France's good economic performance, since its GDP grew at an average of 5.5 percent between 1959 and 1967, with a rate of inflation of 4 percent and a surplus in the balance of trade.[10]

During the second half of the sixties, the development of the events in the international economy indicated that the situation of the monetary system was becoming increasingly complicated, and the gold reserves of the United States kept decreasing. The US government tried to find solutions to alleviate the crisis. In the spring of 1967, it prohibited Germany from using the dollars accumulated because of the surplus of its balance of payments to buy gold, as a condition for the maintenance of unchanged American troop levels in Germany. The Federal Reserve increased the swap lines that it had initiated since the beginning of the sixties with nine central banks (Austria, Belgium, England, France, Germany, Italy, the Netherlands, Switzerland, and Canada), which provided up to $900 million equivalent in foreign exchange. What had started as a small, short-term credit facility grew to be a large, intermediate-term facility. Its growth signaled that these swap lines were not a temporary fix but a sign of a fundamental problem in the monetary system.[11]

However, none of the steps seemed to be working. In mid-1967 the ratio of all liquid American assets to foreign official dollar holdings dropped below 100 percent, and the ratio of its reserve assets to total dollar liabilities to foreign official agencies dropped decisively below 100 percent, which clearly suggested that the United States could not redeem all officially held dollars even using the resources of its private sector.[12] By the final months of 1967, new problems arose because of the serious difficulties of the British pound.

The United States and the IMF supported the British government with large loans, but despite all their efforts, by 1967 Great Britain had lost about 50 percent of its gold reserves. The tense international situation, created as a result of the Six-Day War between Israel and Arab countries and a severe strike of British port workers, caused new fears and complicated the already difficult situation. Finally in November 1967, the pound was devalued from its rate of exchange of 2.80 per dollar, adopted in 1949, to 2.40. I was living in London by that time, and I still remember the headlines of the newspapers in the newsstand near Marble Arch. With their classical British solemnity, they just announced, "Pound devalued." President de Gaulle declared that it was possible "that the problems resulting from the devaluation of the pound could lead to the reestablishment of the international monetary system founded on immutability, impartiality and universality which are the privileges of gold."[13]

These developments put new pressure on the dollar. The buying of gold on the London market peaked at about 250 tons in the five days after the devaluation of the British currency and reached a similar amount in December. The gold pool, which the United States and a group of European countries had organized very early in the sixties to deal with the demand on that market, finally collapsed in March 1968, after the central banks participating in the pool had lost about 12 percent of their reserves in the six months prior to that month.[14] Under the new scenario, central banks no longer supported the market price, and there was a two-tier market. Private transactors could buy and sell at market price, whereas transactions between central banks were placed outside the market, and these continued at the thirty-five-dollar price. Also, the governments agreed that the members of the former pool would not sell gold to replace any central bank sales to the private market. The two-tier agreement remained in effect until November 1973.[15]

On that occasion, the American magazine *Time* published an article that explained the cause of this gold crisis—which actually should be called the dollar crisis—and its meaning for the United States and the rest of the world in very clear and realistic terms:

Most of the reasons for the gold crisis are rooted in the U.S. The country's continuing balance of payments deficit, its constantly out-of-balance domestic budget and its rising outflow of money to finance the *war in Viet Nam are basically responsible for global concern about the soundness of the dollar. Concern has led to the belief that the U.S. would soon have to stop selling gold to all buyers at $35 an ounce and somehow raise the price. The possibility of a price increase touched off the worldwide run on gold...Wall Street regulars took the gold panic with remarkable calm in the knowledge that while the situation could turn into a disaster for the international monetary system, it was unlikely to have a catastrophic effect in the U.S.*[16]

This analysis has the merit of having anticipated what would still take three more years to happen. Its authors realized that those who had the problem were the countries that had trust in the US undertaking to convert dollars into gold at thirty-five dollars an ounce, thus having accumulated large amounts of that currency, while the United States was already so powerful that it could easily relinquish this obligation, and no nation could do anything to make the US fulfill it or take any retaliatory action.

On March 12, 1968, the US Congress abolished the gold reserve requirement of 25 percent gold cover of dollars in circulation. By this action, they definitely removed one of the last links between gold and dollars, so the total gold holdings of the United States could be used to support gold demand.

From its side, in 1969 the IMF created a new reserve asset, the Special Drawing Rights (SDR), which were a new source of liquidity intended to alleviate the pressure on the dollar and gold as the two main reserve assets at that time. The SDR is not a currency like the dollar, the euro, the yen or others. It is a supplementary international reserve asset issued by the IMF and distributed in proportion to the amount of the quotas of its members. Holders of SDRs may obtain other members' currencies in exchange for its SDRs either through voluntary arrangements between them or following the directions of the IMF under certain circumstances. The SDR also serves as the unit of account of the IMF and some other international organizations.

Nevertheless, by 1970 the problems of the international monetary system had become even worse. The United States had lost about half of its official gold reserves, having less than ten thousand tons of this metal left in its reserves. President Nixon's policy to keep the economy expansionary through low interest rates, combined with the anti-inflationary policy of the central bank of Germany *(Bundesbank)*, which kept high interest rates for the German mark, was a recipe of disaster for the dollar.

The selling of dollars in exchange for marks kept growing. At the beginning of May 1971, the Germans tried to persuade principal European countries to agree to a joint float of their currencies, but France and Italy opposed. Under these circumstances, Germany decided to let the mark float, and the Dutch guilder followed it. Switzerland revalued by 7 percent and Austria by 5 percent.

The French government expressed their dissatisfaction with this new outcome of the crisis, criticized the United States for its neglect of the international monetary system, and asserted that Europe needed to find its *own way* in monetary affairs.[17]

The figures of the balance of payments of the United States in the first half of 1971 reaffirmed the pessimistic feeling of the markets. The European press intensified its criticism of the United States, who they thought was not doing enough to find real solutions to the crisis of the monetary system.[18] Foreign central banks experienced large increases in dollar reserves. It was then evident that the United States could not honor its commitment to sell gold at the agreed price of thirty-five dollars. The dollar had become a safe bet for speculators. The question was not *whether* the dollar-gold standard could collapse, but *when* it was likely to happen.

Nixon's Decision of August 15, 1971

In Washington, leaders realized that they were approaching a situation that would force the government to make transcendental and painful

Francisco Soberón

decisions. In a memo from the secretary of the Treasury to President Nixon on June 8, 1971, John Connally revealed the prevailing mood:

The simple fact is that, given our present international economic and financial position, some monetary disturbances—which the press will label "crises"—are virtually inevitable. The test is whether these can be met without impairing our basic domestic (or international) objectives.

Far from "muddling through" the recent disturbance, I believe these essential objectives were maintained:

(1) Quite deliberately, we avoided a strong reaction. By maintaining, insofar as possible, the focus in Europe, we helped deflate concern over a "dollar crisis." Pressures for strong domestic action, either with respect to higher interest rates or strongly intensified controls (or both) never built up.

(2) International sentiment was calmed fairly quickly and effectively in the circumstances.

(3) By making the point that the "crisis" grew most immediately out of domestic German political and economic concerns, we helped limit the repercussions on the dollar and set the stage for maintaining the IMF's role in exercising surveillance over exchange rate practices...

Changes in our present international economic and financial position must be achieved without—and this is the key—undermining confidence in the dollar and the general stability of the monetary system. Should we fail, forces of economic nationalism and isolation in one country after the other—including the United States—could become unmanageable.

I do not underestimate the extent to which the problems are complicated by differing views among economists and businessmen, and among countries. In particular, I believe we must realize there is a strong element of thinking within Europe that would take advantage of weakness or clumsiness on our part to promote the Common Market

86

not as a partner but as a rival economic bloc, competing vigorously with the dollar and reducing or shutting out, as best it can, U.S. economic influence from a considerable portion of the world."[19]

It is interesting to know how the US government was maneuvering to minimize the damage that the events were causing to US interests, by putting the blame on some of their European allies that could benefit from the situation "not as a partner but as a rival economic bloc."

About two month later, on August 2, 1971, in a meeting with President Nixon and other members of the government, Mr. Connally put forward the idea to stop the convertibility of the dollar. Referring to that question, he stressed that "we're going to have to stop that at some point… Everybody, I say 'everybody,' most people tend to think that ten billion dollars [in gold reserves] is the point below which we should not go." [20] In this same meeting, it was mentioned that the United States had lost $850 million in gold reserves in the week of August 2, 1971 alone; that the French had called in over $1 billion in reserves in the previous few weeks; and that the Germans and the Dutch were looking to call in some $200–250 million more.

In order to decide how to proceed in response to this serious crisis, President Nixon and fifteen of his advisers met at the presidential retreat at Camp David between August 13 and 15. The final decision was the most drastic one: the United States would "close the gold window," as they euphemistically described the decision to stop selling gold at the official price of thirty-five dollars per ounce, as had been agreed upon in Bretton Woods.

On August 15 in a television address, the President informed the public of this decision, together with a group of internal steps to fight inflation and stimulate economic growth.

He started by saying that the United States had the best opportunity in that century to achieve two of its greatest ideals: to bring about a full generation of peace and to create a new prosperity without war. He explained that in order to reach that goal, the United States

Francisco Soberón

would need to create more and better jobs, stop the rise in the cost of living, and protect the dollar from the attacks of international money speculators. He then went on to assert that the time had come for a new economic policy for the United States, which would mainly target unemployment, inflation, and international speculation.

He first referred to the problems of unemployment and proposed to create incentives to invest in new machinery and equipment and to approve new tax schemes for stimulating research and development of new industries and new techniques, in order to provide new jobs.

He next mentioned inflation and said that he had decided to freeze all prices and wages throughout the United States for a period of ninety days.

Finally, he addressed the problem that was the real cause of his speech: the dollar crisis. In connection with this, he said that he had to protect the position of the dollar as a pillar of monetary stability around the world. He first heaped blame on speculators, whom he accused of being the only gainers in the financial crisis. He said that because they thrived on crises, they helped to create them. He then explained that in recent weeks the speculators had been waging an all-out war on the American dollar, and he tried to calm fears by assuring that the strength of a nation's currency is based on the strength of that nation's economy—and the American economy was by far the strongest in the world. Then he detonated, without any more delay, what could be defined as a monetary atomic bomb of nineteen words just by saying, "I have directed Secretary Connally to suspend temporarily the convertibility of the dollar into gold or other reserve assets."

Nixon additionally stipulated that in order to protect the dollar and to improve the American balance of payments, the government would impose an additional tax of 10 percent on goods imported into the United States.

He tried to calm down the American people by laying to rest "the bugaboo of what is called devaluation." He took pains to guarantee that to the overwhelming majority of Americans who bought American-made products in America, their dollars would continue to be worth just as much the following day as it was that day. As far as his allies were concerned, he said the following: "To our friends abroad, including the many responsible members of the international banking community who are dedicated to stability and the flow of trade, I give this assurance: The United States has always been, and will continue to be, a forward-looking and trustworthy trading partner."

He finalized his address by reassuring his audience, "Every action I have taken tonight is designed to nurture and stimulate that competitive spirit, to help us snap out of the self-doubt, the self-disparagement that saps our energy and erodes our confidence in ourselves."[21]

Some points about Nixon's decision and address are worth analyzing:

- With only nineteen words, he unilaterally broke the agreement that the US government had reached before the world, to fully back the dollar with gold at a fixed official price, which had been the basis for the *par value system* adopted in Bretton Woods.

- He actually decided to liquidate the international monetary system that had been agreed upon in an international conference twenty-seven years before. The reasonable action would have been to call for an international meeting to reach a new consensus on this subject. Instead of that, President Nixon chose to discuss this matter with a few of his closest advisers and to make a final decision that would shake the world economy. He did not even invite the State Department, which would have to deal with the international reactions of such decisions, to these meeting, since he felt that they looked at the problems from the point of view of other countries.

- His decision had a far-reaching impact on gold prices. The official price of this metal had been $20.67 an ounce from 1834 till 1933 (excluding the period of the American Civil War, from 1861 to 1878), and from 1934 till 1971 it had been $35. This means that the price of gold increased by $14.33 during 137 years. In the new scenario, the situation evolved in such a way that a change of that size could easily occur in weeks and even in one day. Although gold no longer has any monetary function, it is still a reference in the financial markets, so this kind of volatility in its price has influence in the financial markets in general.

• The other steps adopted by Nixon provide a clear example of strict economic regulations by a nation (especially the additional tax of 10 percent on goods imported into the United States), which are precluded from any menu of options in the adjustment programs imposed by the IMF. The United States has complete control over these programs by maintaining a quota and a corresponding voting power of 16.76 percent, while all important decisions have to be decided by a majority of 85 percent.

• As regards the temporary nature of the suspension of gold's convertibility of the dollar, even the most naive person would understand that this step was irreversible, since there were no signs that the events that led to it were likely to disappear in the future.

• The best that could be said of President Nixon's reassurances to his foreign allies is that, under the circumstances, they were very inconsistent. The guarantee that the United States would continue to be *a trustworthy trading partner*, at the moment in which it was unilaterally relinquishing its most important obligation under the prevailing monetary system, had indeed very low moral value.

• As far as the IMF was concerned, it did not take much investigation to realize that the US government totally ignored it in this important decision. Article 1 Paragraph 1 of the Agreement of the IMF, which establishes the purposes of this organization, reads: "To promote international monetary cooperation through a permanent institution which provides the machinery for consultation and collaboration on international monetary problems." According to the content of this article, in order to discuss a *problem* that was causing a crisis in the international monetary system, the nation should have called a meeting of IMF members to analyze and make collective decisions on the subject. Contrary to that, Nixon and a few of his closest advisers made the decision, considering the role of the IMF on this question so unsubstantial that they informed the organization of the *fait accompli* on August 15. Mr. Connally wrote a half-page letter to the managing director of the IMF, just saying, "This is to notify you that, with effect August 15th, 1971 the United States no longer, for the settlement of international transactions, in fact, freely buys and sells gold under the second sentence of Article IV, Section 4 (b)."[22] Probably there have been few cases in history in which a nation has respected the institutional authority of an international organization less than in this case.

• Some authors have made the point that throughout most of the world and most of human history, money was gold, silver, another intrinsically valued commodity, or a claim on such a commodity. It has only been in the most recent four decades, after Nixon's decision, that money flowing around the globe has been claimed on nothing at all.[23] Moreover, his action also ended the long period of fixed exchange rates that had prevailed since the nineteenth century, to open a new scenario that could finally lead to a system of floating exchange rates that could open a new era in the international monetary markets and bring with it new uncertainties.

Finally, Nixon's decision resembles in some way the actions of Dionysius, the tyrant of Syracuse, around 400 BCE. As he had borrowed from his subjects an amount of money that was impossible for him to repay, he ordered all coins in circulation to be handed over to the government upon pain of death. He then reminted the coins and converted every one-drachma coin into a two-drachma coin. By this action, he was then able to pay all his debts in full and keep the same nominal amount of money in circulation. As a matter of fact, Nixon did not appeal to people to return their dollars and did not resort to pain of death. It was neither possible nor necessary. Things were certainly easier for him, as the dollar was not a gold coin but paper representing it. So, he just decided that his money was no longer worth any fixed amount of gold, and by doing this, his obligation to convert dollars to gold ceased to exist one minute after his speech. No doubt, Dionysus would definitely envy the powers of Nixon.

The American Damage-Control Operation

After Nixon's speech, the State Department tried to minimize the negative consequences of a decision that had been taken without consulting any other country, although it had very serious consequences for them. It was not an easy task. Some foreign governments were increasingly upset at the US decision to deal with this problem on a unilateral basis, taking only its own national interest into consideration. A message dated November 15, 1971, from the American Embassy in Paris, describes very well the mood in Europe at the time:

In the last few weeks I have detected a disturbing change in the French attitude. Key French officials have begun to warn us that, if we do not soon indicate clearly what our terms for a settlement are, opinion will turn decisively against us, with incalculable consequences for our political interests in Europe. Our British colleagues have told us they are convinced that, if the next G-10 Ministers' meeting is unproductive, the French will lose hope of reaching an agreement in that forum and will start considering alternative possibilities. Leading financial journalists like Alain Vernay of Le Figaro are increasingly critical in their conversations with Embassy officers of what they describe as US intransigence, and increasingly pessimistic about the future. There have been disturbing signs recently that measures aimed at the multinational corporations are being considered more and more seriously by the French authorities.

The underlying cause of the French malaise is a growing feeling that, by failing to indicate more concretely what our terms for a settlement are, we are blocking a negotiated solution of the crisis. Continued delay in settling the crisis has led to growing uncertainty among French businessmen and is beginning to cause them to defer important investment decisions. The effect the crisis is having on Franco-German relations and on Germany's economic prospects is also a matter of growing concern to the GOF. Behind these immediate concerns lies the deeper fear that if the crisis is not ended soon nations will be increasingly inclined to take defensive measures, with the resulting contraction of world trade leading to a world recession.[24]

As the result of very intense diplomatic efforts, a meeting of the G-10 was held at the Smithsonian Institution in Washington, on December 17 and 18, 1971. The final agreement reached included the realignment of the currencies of the countries of the group against the dollar, including a revaluation of 16.9 percent of the Japanese yen, 13.6 percent of the German mark, and 8.6 percent of the French franc. It was also agreed that the central banks would intervene in the markets selling and buying their currencies to guarantee that the new parities did not change more than 2.25 percent. The United States agreed to devalue the dollar against gold by approximately 8.5 percent, to thirty-eight dollars per ounce.

President Nixon called that agreement "the most significant monetary agreement in the history of the world," forgetting that it meant a strong devaluation of the dollar and that only four months before he had asked the American people and the world "to lay to rest the bugaboo of what is called devaluation."[25]

But the August 15 blow to the Bretton Woods system was a lethal one, and everybody in the political world and the financial markets so understood. During 1972, speculators pushed many European currencies toward the tops of their permissible exchange-rate bands. By intervening, their central banks accumulated large amounts of unwanted dollars.

Gold prices rose to around $60 an ounce by mid-1972 and $90 an ounce by early 1973. On February 12, 1973, with exchange markets in

Europe and Japan closed, the United States devalued the dollar by an additional 10 percent to $42.22 an ounce.

By the middle of 1973, the bands system was abandoned, and all important currencies were left to float freely. The death of the Bretton Woods system could finally be officially decreed.[26] Monetary stability was definitely gone, and a system of floating exchange rates had arrived. That system is still in force in present times.[27] The next chapter will review the problems of such a monetary system.

There is no doubt that the American experts, economists, and politicians who proposed the monetary system that was finally agreed upon in Bretton Woods did not think at the time that it would end in this way. On the other hand, at the moment when Nixon made his decision, it was a fact that the official vaults of the United States did not contain enough gold to maintain the dollar convertibility at the established price. However, it is also clear that once the shock waves had settled down, the United States realized how convenient the new monetary system was to them and how important it was to avoid any new arrangement that could hamper the extraordinary privileges of the dollar in the international monetary system. As the 1999 Nobel Prize winner Robert Mundell ascertained as early as 1976, the traditional method of controlling dollars was through convertibility into primary assets like gold, but the United States felt uncomfortable with this approach if it could lead to a constraint on its monetary policy.[28] It is easy to understand that in these new circumstances the United States did everything it could to ensure that gold could not make a comeback in the international monetary scenario. To that effect it strongly pursued the proposal to eradicate any monetary function of gold, and in 1976 it finally succeeded in obtaining the approval of the second amendment of the IMF. This amendment fundamentally changed the role of gold in the international monetary system, eliminating its use as the common denominator of the post–World War II exchange-rate system and as the basis of the value of the SDR. It also abolished the official price of gold and ended its obligatory use in transactions between the IMF and its member countries. It furthermore required the IMF, when dealing in gold, to avoid managing the price of gold or establishing a fixed price.[29] Therefore, it created all conditions to guarantee the complete hegemony of the dollar as center of the present monetary system, and it is evident that the United States will use all its power to prevent any change that could jeopardize such extraordinary privilege of its currency.

Francisco Soberón

Notes and Bibliography

1)   http://www.oecd.org/general/
themarshallplanspeechatharvarduniversity5june1947.htm. The IMF also describes
the postwar conditions of Europe and Asia in a very vivid way in its exhibit *Money
Matters:* "*By the end of World War II, much of Europe and Asia, and parts of
Africa, lay in ruins. Combat and bombing had flattened cities and towns, destroyed
bridges and railroads, and scorched the countryside. The war had also taken a
staggering toll in both military and civilian lives. Shortages of food, fuel, and all
kinds of consumer products persisted and in many cases worsened after peace
was declared. War-ravaged Europe and Japan could not produce enough goods
for their own people, much less for export.*" *Money Matters, Destruction and
Reconstruction, Part 1* (Washington: International Monetary Fund).

2)   See Robert Triffin, *El caos monetario* (Mexico: Fondo de Cultura
Económica, 1961), 30.

3)   See Stephen G. Hall et al., *Bretton-Woods Systems, Old and New, and
the Rotation of Exchange-Rates* (Leicester: Regimes, University of Leicester,
September 2009), 5–7.

4)   See *The Guardian, Pound devalued 30 %*, September 19, 1949.

5)   See Triffin, *El caos monetario*, 8.

6)   *International Financial Statistics* (Washington: IMF).

7)   See John Kenneth Galbraith, *Money: Whence it came, where it went*
(London: Penguin Books, 1989), 308; Sam Y. Cross, *The Foreign Exchange
Markets in the United States* (New York: Federal Reserve Bank of New York,
1998), 102; Triffin, *El caos monetario*, 33.

8)   Jacques Rueff, *The Monetary Sin of the West* (New York: MacMillan
Company, 1972), 71–73.

9)   Ibid., 78.

10)   Michael David Bordo et al., *An Overplayed Hand: France and the Bretton
Woods International Monetary System* (New Brunswick, NJ: Rutgers University,
1994), 11.

11)   See C. Fred Bergsten, *The Dilemmas of the Dollar* (New York: New York
University Press, 1975), 31–32; Sandra Kollen Ghizoni, *Federal Reserve History*
(Atlanta: Federal Reserve Bank of Atlanta, November 22, 2013).

12)   See C. Fred Bersten, *The Dilemmas of the Dollar*, 150.

13)   Bordo et al., *An Overplayed Hand*, 30.

14)   See Robert Pringle, *The Changing Monetary Role of Gold* (Washington: World Gold Council, 1993), 16.

15)   See Allan H. Meltzer, *U.S. Policy in the Bretton Woods Era* (St. Louis: Federal Reserve Bank of St. Louis, 1991), 73–74.

16)   Time: "Gold at the Point of Panic," Time, March 22, 1968.

17)   See Allan H. Meltzer, *U.S. Policy in the Bretton Woods Era*, 75; Michelle Frasher Rae, *International Monetary Relations between the United States, France, and West Germany in the 1970s* (Texas: A and M University, 2003), 81–83.

18)   *"The foreign press mirrored official concerns. Germany's centre-rightist Die Welt predicted, 'The question no longer is whether the dollar will be devalued, but when and in what way.' The leftist Berlin Telegraf criticized U.S. monetary policy as 'passive and observing. It takes no initiative to restore the health of the international currency system and continues to have the Europeans share the costs of the Vietnam War.' The independent* Times *of London took an international stance— 'It is not exclusively the U.S.'s mess and the U.S. cannot clear it up without the full-hearted cooperation of at least Japan and the Western European powers.' The liberal* Guardian *offered a bleaker view—'The world still seems content to let things drift in the hope that they will improve without radical intervention. It is a vain hope and a dangerous illusion.' By far the most critical reactions came from France. Describing the crisis as the 'collapse of the dollar,' commentators remarked that the dollar should be devalued, but doubted that the U.S. would take the necessary actions so close to an election year. Conservative newspapers warned that France could not let its economy slip to save face for the dollar, and even the moderate* Le Figaro *saw an opportunity for European monetary union. 'The crisis of the currency which serves as a world standard... offers a unique chance of welding the European currencies together, of constituting as of now the European reserve fund contemplated by the Werner plan.'"* Rae, *International Monetary Relations*, 94.

19)   US Department of State, Office of the Historian, *Foreign Relations, 1969–1976, Volume III, Foreign Economic Policy; International Monetary Policy, 1969–1972, Document 158*, archive (Washington).

20)   Scott W. Ohlmacher, *The Dissolution of the Bretton Woods System Evidence from the Nixon Tapes*, August–December 1971 (Newark: University of Delaware, 2009), 6.

21)   See Richard Nixon, "Address to the Nation Outlining a New Economic Policy: 'The Challenge of Peace,'" August 15, 1971, in *The American Presidency Project*, ed. Gerhard Peters and John T. Woolley, http://www.presidency.ucsb.edu/ws/?pid=3115.

22)   Rae, *International Monetary Relations*, 101.

23)   See Benn Steiland and Manuel Hinds, *"Money, Markets, and Sovereignty,"* CFR Book (New Haven, CT: Yale University Press, 2009), 9–10.

24)   US Department of State, *Foreign Relations, Document 197*.

25)   As the British Economist Paul Einzig has explained, devaluation is not a method of defending an exchange but of abandoning its defense. See Paul Einzig, Foreign Exchange Crises (London: MacMillan St. Martin's Press, 1970). Regarding the Smithsonian Agreements, from an historical point of view, to understand the public mood at the time, also consider the comments of the American economist John Kenneth Galbraith to the effect that *"Secretary of the Treasury John B. Connally, who received credit for the agreement, backed momentarily in the esteem which people who do not understand what is happening accord to those who presume to knowledge of money. For both the Smithsonian Agreements and Connally the esteem was short-lived. Both were casualties of the times."* John Kenneth Galbraith, *Money, Whence it came, where it went* (London: Penguin Books, 1975), 310.

26)   Federal Reserve, History: *Smithsonian Agreement* (Washington: November 22, 2013).

27)   Actually, the world enjoyed a long period of stable exchange rates for the most important currencies during the eighteenth and nineteenth centuries and a good part of the twentieth century. For example, the gold value of the French franc set in 1803 was not officially changed until June 25, 1928. Despite slight adjustment, the conversion rate between the French franc and British currencies remained quite stable for two centuries. In the nineteenth and early twentieth centuries, everybody knew that the pound was worth about five dollars, twenty German marks, and twenty-five French francs. See Thomas Piketty, *Capital in the Twentieth-First Century* (Cambridge: The Belknap Press of Harvard University Press, 2014), 104–105.

28)   See Pringle, *Changing Monetary Role*, 29.

29)   See Factsheet, *Gold in the IMF* (Washington: International Monetary Fund, April 9, 2015).

CHAPTER 5

The Present Monetary System and Its Problems

The present monetary system has been operating during the last four decades without any major reorganization. However, it is the source of very serious problems that affect the normal functioning of international economic relations. One could ascertain at least the following five serious flaws of this system, for which there are no possible solutions under the present world monetary order.

Extraordinary volatility. Since the collapse of the Bretton Woods fixed exchange rates, the parity of the most important currencies have fluctuated at unprecedented levels, creating a volatility that hampers commercial and financial activity. Such volatility has a clear impact on emerging market currencies that appreciate or depreciate abruptly, causing all sorts of problems for the governments of these countries, which see how external factors over which they have no control could destroy a correct macroeconomic policy.

Volatility also becomes a source of uncertainty for normal businesses operating in the real economy, since unpredictable and frequent changes in the rates of exchange could cause heavy financial losses and have an important negative impact on a company's results. With the increasing globalization of trade, few entities could totally isolate themselves from this problem. There is no doubt that the present floating-rate system with very volatile exchange rates increases the risks for traders, investors, and others involved in economic activity and makes their decisions more uncertain and difficult.

Countries at the mercy of speculators. Trading in foreign-exchange markets averaged $5.3 trillion per day in 2013. This is up from $4.0 trillion in April 2010, $3.3 trillion in April 2007, and $500 billion in 1989.[1]

To put these figures in context, it should be mentioned that the total volume of exports of goods and services in 2012 equaled about $23 trillion, and the total direct foreign investment was $1.4 trillion, so the total turnover of the foreign-exchange markets in five days exceeded world exports in a year, and one day saw more than the yearly global foreign direct investment.[2]

As a matter of fact, part of this huge upsurge in the daily turnover of the world foreign-exchange markets is due to the increase of foreign exchange risks hedging by companies that operate in the international markets buying and selling goods and services. However, the size, efficiency, and liquidity of these markets make them very convenient and vulnerable for the activity of financial speculators, who are responsible for the major part of the huge volume of the daily transactions. There is no doubt that speculation at great scale in exchange rates has very serious internal consequences, and the events of the last decades have shown that—in view of the size of present speculative operations in the foreign-exchange markets—the governments are usually powerless to avoid its effects, especially in emerging and less developed countries. Governments nowadays have to act in an uncertain environment, as they lack effective tools to respond to such formidable external shocks. It is a fact that speculation on exchange rates has serious and painful internal economic consequences, and domestic policies are relatively powerless to escape them or offset them.[3]

Political leaders, and their opponents, like to pretend that they are still in control of their national economics...But recent years have shown again and again how the politicians' plans have been upset by changes that they could not have foreseen in the world outside the state...The uncertainty that rules in the financial world spills over not only into individual lives but into the fortunes of governments and of countries—and sooner or later into the relations between the states.[4]

International Reserves accumulation. Beyond the basic reasons to hold international reserves—such as the need to deal with balance-of-payment deficits and the risk of having to cope with unexpected financial obligations—the present vulnerabilities in the international monetary system, and the real possibility of exposure to external shocks due to lack of international liquidity and volatility in capital flows, have pushed emerging countries to accumulate huge amounts of foreign-exchange reserves.[5]

In particular, the crisis at the end of the nineties taught a very hard lesson to the governments of the third-world countries that had to resort to the aid of the IMF and accept its tough conditionality and adjustment programs. These governments had to balance the fiscal budget in a short period of time, to liberalize the capital account of the balance of payments, to impose total flexibility in the labor markets, to privatize profitable state-owned entities, etc., and the IMF usually did not take into consideration the specific conditions of the countries where they imposed these programs. As a rule, such programs resulted in a very strong long-term social unrest that actually created more problems than they were supposed to resolve. To avoid the recurrence of such situations, when their external situations improved, mainly because of better prices for their export products, most countries liquidated their debts with the IMF and embarked on very ambitious programs to accumulate reserves. These programs could ensure them enough foreign-exchange resources so that in case of any new external shock they would not have to resort to the IMF aid, which is said to be like the medieval medicine that killed more patients than it saved.

International Reserves (billions of dollars)

Country	1997	2015	
Russia...............	18	376	
Korea...............	20	362	*Source: Data Template on International*
Brazil...............	52	361	*Reserves and Foreign Currency Liquidity,*
India................	28	328	IMF, March 6, 2015.

Persistent imbalances. As explained in Chapter 2, the gold standard system had its own self-correcting mechanism that brings the balance of payments into equilibrium position through the adjustment of money supply and internal prices, and prevents chronic imbalances of international payments. This mechanism could work more or less efficiently, but the fact remains that in some way it provided an instrument to avoid persistent imbalances of the system. In other words, trade imbalances were unsustainable and self-correcting. In the present system, those automatic adjustment mechanisms do not exist. This allows the country that issues the world reserve currency, the United States, to incur chronic deficits of unprecedented magnitude in its balance of payments, without the need to take steps to correct them. It also allows its creditor countries to accumulate large amounts of international reserves, which can cause financial disruptions. It has been widely acknowledged that the dollar dominance allows the United States to live beyond its means and some countries have strongly criticized such "exorbitant privilege" enjoyed by the United States.

Many knowledgeable authors have pointed out that this is an unsustainable situation. They argue that "as long as the US keeps spending more than it earns, trade and budget deficits will persist which will push the US government debt-to-GDP ratio as well as the US external debt-to-GDP ratio to such high levels that at some point this will undermine confidence in the US dollar, much as it did in the late 1960s which led to the breakdown of the gold exchange standard and brought an end to the fixed exchange rate system. If this imbalance is allowed to persist to that level, instead of an orderly depreciation in the value of the Greenback we might see a new monetary crisis."[6]

On the other hand, the consequences of these imbalances are equally problematic for the countries with continuous surpluses in the current account balance of payments. The following report from Reuters indicated the worries of the Chinese authorities regarding the extraordinary increase of China's international reserves as a consequence of such surpluses:

China's war chest of foreign currency reserves has become a headache as its continued rise could stoke inflation in the long term, Premier Li Keqiang said in remarks seen on Sunday, pledging to reduce the country's trade surplus. China's foreign exchange reserves, the world's largest, grew by $130 billion in the first quarter, to a record $3.95 trillion... "Frankly speaking, foreign exchange reserves have become a big burden for us, because such reserves translate into the base money, which could affect inflation," Phoenix New Media Ltd quoted Li as saying during a visit to Kenya. Large foreign currency purchases by China's central bank, which regularly intervenes to cap Yuan rises, amount to creation of base money and can fuel inflation unless the central bank soaks up the excess Yuan injected into the system.[7]

US policy determines global liquidity. After President Nixon's decision to end the convertibility of dollars into gold, the United States could finance its external deficits just by endlessly incurring debts in its own currency. Under such a monetary system—with the dollar as the main reserve currency and the dominant international medium of payment—global liquidity depends on the macroeconomic policies and balance-of-payments imbalances of the United States, which can result in either excessive or limited world liquidity, creating serious problems in most of the countries of the world. It should be noted that the role of the dollar in the international monetary system exceeds the share of the United States in the global economy. Whereas the GDP of this country is about 25 percent of the world GDP, deals with the dollar on one side of the transactions in the foreign-exchange markets represent 87 percent of all deals. The US share of bank notes held overseas is 65 percent, and the dollar accounts for 62 percent of the international foreign-exchange reserves.[8]

The last decades have seen patterns of growing deficits in the American external accounts, which have created huge amounts of liquidity that have flooded the world, causing credit bubbles and asset price inflation. In connection with this, it should be noted that in the thirty years following the collapse of the Bretton Woods system, the

United States incurred a cumulative deficit of about three trillion dollars, whereas its external imbalances grew to such an extent that a total deficit of a similar size was incurred only in the period between 2005 and 2008.[9]

To make things worse, US policy regarding its external accounts and the resulting global liquidity has usually been unpredictable, and in the last instance the US has decided that policies "with little consideration of their impact on global aggregate demand or demands for global liquidity are thus a potential cause of instability in exchange rates and global activity."[10]

Notes and Bibliography

1)   Bank for International Settlements, *Triennial Central Bank Survey, Foreign exchange and derivatives market activity,* Basle 2007, 2010 and 2013.

2)   United Nations Conference on Trade and Development (UNCTAD), World Investment Report (Genève: 2013); *World Trade Organization,* "Press Release" (Genève: April 14, 2014).

3)   See James Tobin, *A proposal for international monetary reform* (New Haven, CT: Cowles Foundation, Yale University, 1978), 3.

4)   Susan Strange, *Casino Capitalism* (Manchester: Manchester University Press, 1997), 3.

5)   See *Reserve Accumulation and International Monetary Stability* (Washington: International Monetary Fund, April 13, 2010), 5. See also *The Post-American World*, where its author points out the shifts from the 1990s, when the East Asian nation desperately needed the IMF to bail them out of their crisis, to now, when they are using massive foreign-exchange reserves to finance American debt. Fareed Zacaria, *The Post-American World* (New York: W. W. Norton and Company, 2008), 217–218.

6)   Kenneth Matziorinis, *A Brief History of the International Monetary System* (Montreal: McGill University, 2006), 26. See also Esward Prasad, *The Dollar Reigns Supreme, by Default,* (New York: International Monetary Fund, 2014).

7)   "China's FX reserves may stoke inflation, a 'big burden': Premier," Reuters, May 11, 2014.

8)   Bank for International Settlements, *Triennial Central Bank Survey, 2013; Currency Composition of Official Foreign Exchange Reserves (COFER), 2015 and Reserve Accumulation and International Monetary Stability* (Washington: International Monetary Fund, April 13, 2010), 8.

9)   See Richard Duncan, *The Dollar Crisis* (Singapore: John Wiley and Sons (Asia) Pte. Ltd., 2003), 12.

10)   United Nations, "Report of the Commission of Experts of the President of the United Nations General Assembly on Reforms of the International Monetary and Financial System" (New York: September 21, 2009), 110.

EPILOGUE

I feel that the serious flaws of the present monetary system and its background have been clearly demonstrated in the present text. Furthermore, there is already certain consensus on the idea that the system should be reformed in order to contribute to the efficient functioning of the international economic system and avoid the uncertainties that characterize it. However, when it comes time to prescribe the best solution, the ideas are far from unanimous, and the proposals are diverse and of different natures. These include creating a global central bank; issuing a world currency; controlling capital flows; coordinating macroeconomic policies; founding an international credit-insurance corporation; fixing the euro-dollar exchange rate within wide limits, with interventions of the ECB and the Federal Reserve to keep it within the limits agreed; giving the SDR a greater role to act as a super-sovereign reserve currency; and entrusting the IMF with part of the reserves of its member countries to be centralized and managed by this organization.[1]

In any case, one thing is clear: this is not the kind of problem that could be solved unilaterally, and any real solution would require the concerted efforts of most of the states of the world, especially those having the strongest and most important economies. During World War II, the allied governments held consultations regarding the international monetary system that should be adopted after the end of the war. That finally led them to meet at the Bretton Woods Conference in July 1944 and to agree upon the system that could be in force after the end of the hostilities. That system collapsed in 1971, and it has not been replaced by any other monetary arrangements commonly agreed upon.

Under the present circumstances, the most reasonable steps could be to organize consultations among the main countries, to organize an international conference to discuss the present problems of the international monetary system, and to agree upon new alternatives that could lead to an orderly reorganization that would reflect the new world-economy realities and requirements. The Report of the Commission of Experts of the President of the United Nations General Assembly on Reforms of the International Monetary and Financial System in June and September 2009 was a remarkable effort in that direction, but, regretfully, it did not find enough support from the most important countries to be the basis for such an international conference with decision-making powers.

In any case, as the global crisis that started in 2007 demonstrated, the present monetary system is inherently weak; it does not contribute to the normal functioning of international economic relations, and if no action is taken, it is likely to cause new turbulence that could lead to new severe and profound crises.[2] Few would disagree with this conclusion. The question is whether the international community will act in a timely manner to coordinate the actions requested for a reasonable reform of the present monetary system or, on the contrary, nothing will be done and the world will risk a disorderly and abrupt collapse of this system at a time and at a cost that nobody could predict.

Notes and Bibliography

1)   See among others C. Fred Bergsten, *The Dilemmas of the Dollar* (New York: New York University Press, 1975); Robert Guttmann, *The International Monetary System in Transition* (New York: 1998); Robert Mundell, *International Monetary Reform 2011* (Nanjing: Columbia University, China G-20 Seminar, March 31, 2011); United Nations, *Report of the Commission of Experts of the President of the United Nations General Assembly on Reforms of the International Monetary and Financial System* (New York: September 21, 2009); Richard Duncan, *The Dollar Crisis* (Singapore: John Wiley and Sons (Asia) Pte. Ltd., 2003); James Tobin, *A Proposal for International Monetary Reform* (New Haven, CT: Cowles Foundation, Yale University, 1978); Zhow Xiaouchuan, "Reform the International Monetary System," 2009, http://www.chinaview.cn.

2)   *"The turbulence in world financial markets strikes me as a test—of cooperative economic leadership in a world rapidly integrating economically and with dispersed political power and decision making. I do not underestimate the difficulty of the challenge. But, with the danger so clear, the crisis affords opportunities for monetary reforms that have for so long been neglected."* Paul A. Volcker, *The Sea of Global Finance, Global Capitalism* (New York: The New Press, 2000), 85.

Even outstanding speculators that benefit from the flaws of the present monetary system realize that: *"It is time to recognize that financial markets are inherently unstable. Imposing market discipline means imposing instability, and how much instability can society take? Market discipline needs to be supplemented by another discipline: Maintaining stability in the financial markets ought to be an explicit objective of public policy."* See George Soros, *The Crisis of Global Capitalism* (New York: Public Affairs, 1998). 176.